The One Dollar A Day Millionaire

Lucky Vincent

Copyright © 2017 Lucky Vincent

All rights reserved.

ISBN-10:1542778719
ISBN-:13-978-1542778718

DEDICATION

Especially dedicated to all pioneer members of the One Dollar A Day Millionaire's Club, Port Harcourt, Nigeria, through whom the ideas presented in this book were first tested before the book was written

INTRODUCTION

Virtually everybody in the world wants to be a millionaire. But not everybody knows what it takes to be a millionaire. And some who know what it takes to be a millionaire are not willing or ready to give it what it takes. Hence they remain poor despite their desire to become millionaires.

What does it take to be a millionaire? Certainly, becoming a millionaire is not an easy task. It is, in fact, an uphill task. If not, everybody would have become a millionaire. But the fact that there are fewer people in the world who are millionaires than those who are not is a proof that becoming a millionaire is a Herculean task. But, sure, it is a task that can be done. And that is why we have millions, if not billions, of people who have gone from acute poverty to become even multi-millionaires. And if those people could become millionaires, it means that anybody can become a millionaire. But that person must be ready and willing to give it what it takes. So, what does it take to be a millionaire? Like every other attainment in life, it takes a number of factors or traits to become a millionaire.

Life is a game that requires the fighting spirit. Winning, in virtually every game in life, is never easy to come by. In fact, we have more quitters in virtually every game than winners. To emerge a winner in any game, you need very strong determination to keep on keeping on till you win. You need the die-hard or never-say-die spirit to keep at it to the end. This is what is called the fighting spirit. You need to have it because nothing good comes easy. In life, nobody gets anything on a platter of gold. Everybody must fight to get what he wants. To give up at any time is to lose out and never to have what you desire in life. But to hold on and hold out is to take the chance of winning and receiving the laurels that you want in life.

And as far as the issue of becoming a millionaire is concerned, nobody becomes one without a fighting spirit. Authorities and experts have established that over 80% of the world's millionaires arose from poor lower class families. What is responsible for this is that these people have a very strong fighting spirit – that is responsible for propelling them and lifting them out of the dungeon of poverty to the realm of great wealth. Thus the fighting spirit is an indispensable requirement for wealth building. It is this spirit that will enable you to work and keep working, strive and keep striving, give and keep giving, save and keep saving, invest and keep investing, pray and keep praying, believe and keep believing until you arrive at great wealth, and until you move from a nonentity to a celebrity in life.

Life is all about gallantry. No timid, chicken-hearted person goes to the warfront and comes back alive. Only gallant soldiers are allowed to go to the warfront. Life is a battlefield, and the battle, most often, is very fierce; and it takes gallantry to pull through and survive the battles of life. The battle is even fiercer in the issues of wealth and wealth accumulation. It is in fact one of the hottest warfronts. It is so hot that millions have ended up as casualties in the course of battling for money. This is why you must have all it takes to fight and emerge a winner in this game; I mean this battle. And one major requirement is gallantry; that is, bravery or intrepidity. Without it, no soldier ventures into and survives any battle, let alone win victory in it.

Seriously speaking, becoming a millionaire is a game of numbers. A millionaire is simply a person who has accumulated a monetary net worth of up to seven digits of any country's currency, such as N1,000,000 or $1,000,000 or £1,000,000 or €1,000,000. What this means is that the moment a person has acquired or accumulated the first one million of the country's currency, that person is qualified to be called a millionaire. And being able to earn, acquire, gather or accumulate one million of a country's currency is what the war about becoming a millionaire is all about.

Ideally, any fool can become a millionaire. But that is the ideal situation. The real fact of life is that about 95% of the world's population, from the ages past to the present, have not been able to achieve this feat, as simple as it seems. A large majority of the people in the world have ended up far below the millionaire target. And this is rather unfortunate and both disheartening and very discouraging.

So, the question that readily and perpetually hangs on every lip is, is it so difficult to become a millionaire? And the answer to this is, NO! Becoming a millionaire is not as difficult as it seems. It is a matter of understanding that it is a game of numbers. It is as simple as knowing the first number with which you begin to count up to 1,000,000. And the first number, as you can see here, is 1. What this means is that once you begin to count from 1 and you do not stop counting, you are sure to get to 1,000,000. And beginning to count is to earn, acquire and set aside the first coin or currency note in your journey towards becoming a millionaire. For, as has been strongly said by Robert Schuller, beginning is half done; which means that once you have taken the first step towards becoming a millionaire, the others will naturally follow.

The sole reason why many people have not achieved the feat of becoming millionaires is because they have not taken the first step. Becoming a millionaire is not as lofty, difficult and scary as that. All that you have to do is to face your fears and eat that frog, as Brian Tracy would say. All that you have to do is to reduce or belittle the mountain and climb it from the bottom up.

Life is a game of numbers; and becoming a millionaire is just a game of numbers. But it is a game that you must be willing to play. Nobody wins a game that he is not involved in, no matter how much interest he has in the game. Majority of people in the world are mere spectators in the millionaires' game. They are only watching the very few people who are playing the game. Some are so intrigued by the game that they have joined the fans club to clap hands for and cheer up those who are playing the game. Some others have even graduated to become financial, investment or economic analysts for the millionaires' game. But the sad thing is that these very enthusiastic spectators, fans and analysts are not involved in playing the game, hence they remain poor, year in year out, while those who are playing the game are growing richer and richer every day. And this is really very sad.

The only way to become a millionaire is to get involved in playing the millionaires' game. It is the game of making money; it is the game of saving money; it is the game of investing money; it is the game of making your money to work for you; and above all, it is the game of numbers, which showcases the miracle of compound interest. Get involved in this game; it works wonders!

Whether anybody knows it or not, money is the oil that lubricates the world (the human society) in which man operates. Hence, if you have the knowledge of God, the Creator of the world and of man who lives in it; if you have the knowledge of man, the operator (or manager) of the world; if you have the knowledge of the world, the resources around the world; and you lack the knowledge of money, the oil (or fluid) that enables the resources to flow freely, you will most likely have great difficulties in getting things organized to achieve your desired goals or to realize your desired dreams. Hence, with all your getting, get understanding or the knowledge of money in order to make things work for you.

But we have a faulty education system in which nobody taught or teaches you about money. Yet, understanding money – what it is, how it works, how to make it work for you, how to earn it, and how to keep it – is absolutely essential to your life, your relationships, your world, your happiness and your future. To exclude the knowledge of money from your education is to exclude you from the best that life has to offer. Above all, learning how to become financially successful is one of the most critical skills that you must seek to acquire.

And as we said earlier, money skill is not taught at school or at any other designated institution in the world. Hence, everyone must bear his own burden here. Fortunately for us, in addition to the Holy Bible that has some exposure on money, many self help books have been written by men who have learnt from experience and by the rule of thumb (in fact many of them, including me, got their fingers burnt in the process). It therefore behooves a man of wisdom to seek out the Bible and some of such books on money (including this one), and seek out a quiet place, to read, learn and acquire the knowledge of money, the fourth of the most important areas of knowledge that man needs to have in order to perform optimally in life.

The international monetary community has established a thin line that demarcates between the poor and the rich. It is called, The Poverty Line, which is defined by one dollar a day. What this means is that, anyone who is earning and living below one dollar a day is internationally regarded as a very poor person. This also means that a person is wealthy to the level that he is able to rise above the poverty line. In this connection, the international monetary community has observed that, unfortunately, majority of people in the world are living below the poverty line; hence majority of people on earth are poor, and are living in acute poverty.

What has just been said above is not the complete story. The true story is that people are poor not only because they earn and live below the poverty line; rather, a large majority of people are poor because they conserve nothing for the purposes of investment and wealth building. Many of these people earn and live well above the poverty line but still remain poor. For instance, virtually all middle level income earners earn and live above one dollar a day, yet very many of them are very poor. Even, most business people, including petty traders make profits and live above the dollar a day, yet many of them are very poor. So, what is responsible for people being very poor is not really because they earn and live below the poverty line; rather, it is because they spend or consume all that they earn. And this is the true story of majority of people living on the planet earth today.

The unalloyed truth is that you can become wealthy to the level that you are able to earn and save above the poverty line. This means that until you are able to save and invest at least one dollar a day from your earnings, your struggle with poverty continues. You must therefore resolve to join the minority of people who are able to rise above the poverty line to become wealthy. And it begins with your having the determination to save and invest a minimum of one dollar a day – every day – for the rest of your life.

So, rising above the poverty line begins with earning and saving above the dollar or its equivalents. It requires you to form the habit of saving consistently and persistently. It requires you to make a rock-solid decision to save and invest a part of the money that enters your hand. It requires you to know that any money that comes to you has two divisions, each serving a specific purpose.

The goal of this book is to give you some financial education and to get you to change your attitude towards money and how to save and invest it. If I can get you to form the habit of saving and investing at least one dollar a day, I would have achieved my aim of writing this book, and I would be fulfilled as having impacted you and your future generations.

CONTENTS

Acknowledgments	i
Dedication	ii
Introduction	iv
1. Any Fool Can Become Rich	3
2. What It Takes to Be A Millionaire	6
3. It's A Game of Numbers	23
4. 4 Most Essential Knowledge in Life	45
5. What You Must Know about Money	51
6. How to Rise above the Poverty Line	58
7. Charting Your Way to Wealth: Borrowing & Lending	67
8. Principles of Wealth Creation in Business	82
9. Essentials of Customer Service	116
10. 3 Cornerstones for Building Great Wealth	149
11. The Purpose of Prosperity	170
12. It's A Covenant Walk	179

ACKNOWLEDGMENTS

First, I give glory to God for His inspiration and strength, and for seeing me through the writing and publishing of this book.

My sweetheart and darling wife, Emmanuella, and our lovely kids, Michael, Deborah and David, deserve my unreserved and heartfelt appreciation for the love, warmth, understanding, support, prayers and patience they have always demonstrated towards me and my writing career.

I also acknowledge all my loved ones, especially my Mum, Madam Ruth Kuti; my brothers, Mr. Christopher Obobolo, Dr. Amos Obobolo, Mr. Major Obobolo, Barr. Oviemuno (Brown) Obobolo and Mr. Samuel (a.k.a. Bonny) Ovoro; my sisters, Late Mrs. Queen Egwero, Mrs. Janet Adurosakin, Mrs. Helen Atomah, Angelina, Hannah and Faith; not forgetting all other members of the Obobolo, Idume, Egboro and Akpore families of Aviara, in Isoko South Local Government Area of Delta State, Nigeria.

I also appreciate the encouragement and support of the Management and staff of the Grundtvig International Secondary School, Oba, Delta State Polytechnic, Ozoro, University of Port Harcourt, Port Harcourt and all those who contributed in one way or the other towards the success of this book project.

I pray that God will adequately reward you all for contributing liberally towards the development of the human society.

1

Any Fool Can Become Rich

There is no disputing the fact that in any issue of life, wisdom is the principal thing that you need. You are therefore enjoined to get wisdom among all other gettings in life. (Proverbs 4:7). But do you know that it takes foolishness to become rich and wealthy, and that any fool can become a millionaire? Yes, this really is a paradox of life, but it is true!

It is difficult to believe, but do you know that the most valuable things of life come through foolishness? Now, let us start with God. For Him to reconcile the world to himself, He had to first come down in human flesh to die in the hands of men! Does that make any sense? Then take the case of Jesus Christ; for Him to become the first born among many brethren, He had to give His own life first. Also, consider the man Abraham; for him to become the father of multitudes of children, he had to sacrifice his heir apparent first. Do any of these scenarios look like display of wisdom?

Can you imagine that it takes the foolishness of preaching to get people saved? (1 Corinthians 1:18-29). Then think about the corn of wheat; it does not multiply unless it first falls to the ground and dies. In other words, for your corn of wheat to multiply, you must first lose it by allowing it to leave your hands, which implies that if you choose to hold on to your corn of wheat and you refuse to let it go, that is the only thing you will ever have – it will abide alone. But if you let it go, it will bring forth much fruit.

This is also the way to wealth. Wealth (money) does not increase if you hold unto it. If you like, keep your money under your pillow and be watching it closely; or bury it at the centre of your bedroom or at any secret place where nobody else can have access to it; and bring it out after 50 years. That money will not only remain the same quantity of it that you kept there, but it would have greatly depreciated in value due to the effect of inflation; and your wisdom of keeping your money would have indeed turned to foolishness.

For you to make your money to appreciate in value and therefore multiply in quantity is for you to release it from your hands. This, indeed, is foolishness turned inside out, because it takes the foolishness of losing your money for you to find it again at a higher value later. The reason for this is that your hands may not be competent enough to increase or multiply the value or quantity of your money. You must therefore learn to put your money into the hands of those people who are skilled and competent enough to help make your money grow and multiply for you. This is what we do when we save or invest our money in banks, cooperative societies, or in other investment/financial houses or even in the kingdom of God.

For you to give your money to other people to trade with on your behalf, you must have some element of trust for the people you are entrusting your money with. If you are not ready to trust anybody with your money, then you are not ready to increase or multiply your wealth. This is because, every business, and indeed every investment is based on trust. When you order for goods and they are delivered to you before payment, your suppliers are trusting that you will make payment on receipt of the goods. When you pay for items before they are supplied or delivered to you, you trust the producers or sellers to deliver on their promise. When you sign a contract and move to site immediately to commence operation without mobilization, you trust the contractee to keep to the terms of the contract. So you must have to trust people for you to do business with them. And, on this, everybody has to play the fool.

You must trust people for you to become a millionaire. And trusting people is inversely proportional to the risk of being swindled or played a fool. Of course, there are so many bad people in this world, but you must believe that we have some good people too. You must believe that not all men are fraudsters. This is what will enable you to entrust your money into the hands of those people that you think you can trust, either for safe-keeping or for profitable investment or trading activities. In other words, for your money to increase or multiply in quantity or appreciate in value, you must be ready to play the fool. If not, be ready to permanently remain the poor man that you are.

2

What It Takes to Be a Millionaire

Virtually everybody in the world wants to be a millionaire. But not everybody knows what it takes to be a millionaire. And some who know what it takes to be a millionaire are not willing or ready to give it what it takes. Hence they remain poor despite their desire to become millionaires.

What does it take to be a millionaire? Certainly, becoming a millionaire is not an easy task. It is, in fact, an uphill task. If not, everybody would have become a millionaire. But the fact that there are fewer people in the world who are millionaires than those who are not is a proof that becoming a millionaire is a Herculean task. But, sure, it is a task that can be done. And that is why we have millions, if not billions, of people who have gone from acute poverty to become even multi-millionaires. And if those people could become millionaires, it means that anybody can become a millionaire. But that person must be ready and willing to give it what it takes.

So, what does it take to be a millionaire? Like every other attainment in life, it takes a number of factors or traits to become a millionaire. In this chapter, we want to consider some of the factors or traits that a person must possess in order to become a millionaire.

Desire

To rise out of poverty to become a millionaire demands having a very strong desire. If you do not have a strong enough desire to become a millionaire, you very likely will give up very soon in the face of the great challenges that will confront you from time to time. You will most likely begin to take things easy and relapse to the complacency that has made you remain in poverty all the while.

Have a very strong desire to become a millionaire at all costs. Have a desire not to remain poor in life, for whatever reasons. Have a desire to join the adorable league of millionaires who are making tremendous impact in the human society.

Passion/Drive

In addition to having a strong desire to become a millionaire, you must also have a strong passion for the realization of your goal to become a millionaire. Passion is stronger than desire. It is a very strong, deeply felt emotion for what you desire. Passion gives force or impetus to desire. To become a millionaire, you must not only have passion for money, but you must also have great passion to get out of poverty to become a millionaire. Nothing short of this will see you through to realizing your dream of becoming a millionaire.

Determination

Determination is another force that you must have and apply to your task of becoming a millionaire. Determination is the ability to continue trying to achieve what you have decided to do even when it proves very difficult. Really, becoming a millionaire is a very difficult task. But you must be determined to give it all it takes to become one. Determination is what will enable you to follow through to the realization of your vision, comes what may.

Be strongly determined to get out of the dungeon of poverty into the palace of wealth. Be strongly determined to get out of the group of the wretched of the earth to be counted among the millionaires of the world. Make your goal of becoming a millionaire a task that must be done at all costs. A dogged determination is what it takes to become a millionaire that the world will celebrate.

Decision

Until you decide for something, you are not yet decided. Very many people want to become millionaires, but they have not made that clear-cut decision to become millionaires. Until you definitely decide to be a millionaire, your desire to become a millionaire will be among those numerous and insatiable human wants that may not be realized. Your want becomes converted into a need through decision. What this means is that you really need to choose to be a millionaire to become one. When you have not chosen or decided to be a millionaire, you will have the tendency to pursue your dream half-heartedly and thereby make it a probability. But when you make the definite decision or choice to become a millionaire, then you do not merely have a dream, but a goal that you want to reach with certainty. So decide to be a millionaire and you will surely become one. The reason is that, you become whoever or whatever you choose to become. There is no doubt about this!

Purpose

Nothing is done without a purpose. For you to desire to become a millionaire, you must have a purpose for it. Therefore, if you are yet to determine the purpose for your wealth, then you must do so immediately. For it has been said that when the purpose of a thing is unknown, abuse is inevitable. And this is the reason why many people who suddenly come about great wealth abuse it in wanton abandon.

Your purpose is your motivation; it is what drives you to do what you are doing. Show me a man who sluggishly drags his feet in doing what he is doing, and I will show you a man who has no purpose for doing what he is doing. On the other hand, show me a man who is so determined, daring, undaunted, enthusiastic, agile and excited about what he is doing, and I will show you a man with a great purpose. When you look at people walking along the pedestrian ways, it is easy to identify those who have purposes burning in their hearts and those who do not. Those with purposes are the people who raise their heads, look up and straight with confidence and take good steps and walk briskly in pursuit of their assignments. But those without purposes are most probably those people who are never in a hurry, but stroll languidly, looking down, or at people or things or happenings around and with the look of uncertainty, confusion or perplexity visibly written upon their faces.

Purposeless people are habitually lethargic in what they do. And the reason is obvious: it is your purpose that determines your pursuits; and it is your motive that determines your motivation.

So, what is your purpose for wanting to become a millionaire? If your purpose is not great or good enough, then you will most probably not be spirited enough to pursue the purpose. The greatness of your purpose determines the greatness of the steps you take in pursuit of the purpose. Hence, the greater the purpose, the greater the steps or strides; and the quicker too! Also, the quality of your purpose determines the quality of your pursuit of the purpose. If your purpose is not good, noble or pure enough, you will most probably not give it the best or hot chase. You will most probably pursue it half-heartedly and haphazardly. Therefore you must ensure that you have a good and pure purpose by purifying it; and you can do so by placing it side by side or by filtering it with the word of God. If the purpose for your wealth is a selfish one – for you to accumulate money to feed your lusts, pride and ego – then it is an impure purpose. But if, on the other hand, your purpose of becoming wealthy is so you can live a more fulfilled life, be a blessing to people, contribute to the improvement of humanity and, most importantly, to the building of God's kingdom, then you have a pure purpose. Consequently, when your purpose is impure, it becomes unrealistic, and you become insatiable, and you end up in frustration. On the other hand, when your purpose is pure, you become contented with what you have per time, and you end up fulfilled in life. Please purify your purpose, and you will live happily ever after.

Vision

Until you see it, you cannot have it. This is a biblical principle of life. Vision is your ability to see where you are going and what you are going to find there. If you cannot see it, you cannot get it. If you see nothing, you get nothing. If you see little, you get little. If you see plenty, you get plenty. It is what you see that you get. This principle is applicable to everything and to every issue of life.

If becoming a millionaire is what you desire, then you must begin to see yourself as one. If you cannot see yourself as a millionaire now, then you can never become one later. If you see yourself as a poor man now, then you will not be otherwise tomorrow, you will still be a poor man. And this is the greatest undoing of many people in our societies today. Many people around us would say, "Don't worry, I may be poor today, but you will see what I will become tomorrow." And my response to that is, "If you see yourself as a poor man today, then you will still be a poor man tomorrow." This is what is called 'poor man's mentality'; meaning, when you have a poor man's mentality, you remain poor today and always; but when you have a 'rich man's mentality', you become rich both now and ever. Therefore, what can you see about yourself? Are you seeing a poor man or a rich man? Are you seeing a hundrednaire, a thousandnaire, or a millionaire?

And talking about being a millionaire, still, it is what you see that you get. If you see yourself as managing to at least make a million naira before you die, that is exactly what you will get – one million naira – and nothing more. But if, instead, you see yourself as becoming, not just a millionaire, but a multi-millionaire, of course, that is what you will get. And if you are daring enough to see yourself becoming a billionaire or even a trillionaire, there is no doubt about it; that is what you will get. Nothing is out of reach in this life. It all depends on your ability to see it. If indeed you can see it, then you can get it. Go, and expand your vision – as far as your eyes can see!

Skill/Talent

Skill is a major requirement for anyone who desires to become a millionaire. Apart from the fact that the person must be skillful in handling and managing money, he must be such a person that has a skill that he can convert to cash. This is why it is necessary for everyone to acquire some skills in addition to the general education that you may have. The world no longer belongs to holders of impressive certificates and intimidating curriculum vita. The world now belongs to skillful and talented people. So you better bring out that latent skill or talent of yours, hone it and begin to employ it towards your financial independence.

What I am saying here is that you should find a hobby in your skill, talent or natural ability; then convert that hobby into a business, a product or service, or into a money making venture. Look for that thing that you know how and love to do very well and begin to do it, not only to catch fun, but also to make money. And you don't necessarily have to remain with only those old skills of yours, commit to learning and acquiring new skills periodically and regularly. This is imperative because the world is changing very fast and new ways of doing things (i.e. new skills) are emerging every day in proportion, and with the same rapidity, to the changing world. Therefore to catch up with the frequent changes in the world, you must regularly develop or acquire new skills that are required by the changes, so as to continue to be relevant in the scheme of things. Failure to do this is to risk becoming obsolete and being left behind in this progressive world.

As I hinted earlier, apart from the need to regularly develop or acquire new skills, hone your talents and natural abilities for practical application to the business of making money. You also need to have, acquire or develop the skill of handling or managing money. The greatest and most perilous illiteracy we have in the world today is financial illiteracy. I don't know how and why and for whose interest, but most probably for selfish interests and inordinate ambitions, world leaders and administrators have succeeded in establishing an educational system that teaches people nothing about money. Hence, almost 100% of people in the world know very little or next to nothing about how money works. And this is evident in the acute poverty and heavy indebtedness that individuals, organizations, and nations are suffering all over the world today.

The only solution to this global challenge is the emergence or evolution of new and selfless world leaders and administrators who will help establish a functional educational system that teaches, along with other areas of the school curriculum, how money works and how to handle and manage it. This really is a tall dream and order, especially considering the kind of leaders and administrators that we have in the world today. So, rather than wait for such an utopian and egalitarian society and a functional system of education that may never become a reality, why not start your own process of acquiring financial education? Even if they didn't teach you at school how money works and how it is handled and managed, you can as well be taught at home or at a special business school or financial institution or you can engage the services of consultants or by patronizing and learning from experts through books, tapes, CDs, DVDs, the Internet, seminars, workshops, symposia, conferences, etc. In this age of Information Technology where information on every conceivable subject is available at your finger tips and could be accessed merely by a soft touch, you really have no excuse, but to engage in the process of acquiring the knowledge of how money works and the skill of handling and managing it. This you must do immediately if really you are serious about becoming a millionaire!

Boldness/Risk Taking

It is an established fact that entrepreneurship is risk taking. This means that every business person is a risk taker. By implication, every business person is an investor and every investment involves risk. As you put your money into that business or investment opportunity, there is high probability that you may lose your money or part of the money; there is high probability that you may barely break even and recoup your capital without making any profit; there is also high probability that you may make huge profit or small profit. There is no absolute guarantee or iron-clad assurance in the business and investment world. Hence, every businessman or investor who desires to become a millionaire or have great wealth must first be a risk taker.

However, you don't necessarily have to be a businessman or an investor before you become a risk taker. In fact, everybody in life is a risk taker. At every point in life, whatever we do or don't do, whatever we say, wherever we go, whatever choice or decision we make or do not make, whatever step we take or refuse to take and whatever activity we engage in or refuse to engage in, all entail risk taking. You may succeed or fail, lose or win. Such is the game of life.

Thus, not risking or not willing to take any risk in life is, in itself, very risky. It has far reaching consequences. You may end up stagnated, stranded, demoted, frustrated and retarded. You may end up a failure, a vegetable, an invalid or even a corpse in a coffin or grave. It is very risky not to take risk. Nothing ventured, nothing succeeds.

And if becoming a millionaire or super wealthy is what you desire in life, then you must have or develop the boldness to take risks. You must not be timid, but be bold in making decisions, taking steps, making moves or going into action. But risk has to be taken with great care. Don't take any risk just for the fun of taking risk. Don't take any risk just because you are pressurized to do or say something. Take your time to first do your homework and be sure that the risk is worth taking. As a businessman or as an investor, you are not doing things for people to hail you or clap for you; you are doing things because you want to make profit. So before you venture into any business or investment, be absolutely sure that you will recover your capital and also make substantial profit. If not, don't take the risk. In a nutshell, take only calculated risks. What this means is that you should do your calculations and be certain that you have good profit margin before you commit your money into the business or investment. Be wise!

Trust

Much as it is important for you to be sure of the person(s) you deal or relate with, you must also know that there are no absolutes in life, and there are few saints in the world. Man is not an angel. Hence we have all kinds of human beings in the world. We have the good, the bad and the ugly in the human society. Therefore you should be ready to encounter and deal with different characters as you get on the stage to play your part in the game of life.

Man, in his raw Adamic state, is naturally depraved and has a natural tendency or propensity to do evil. Hence you must get a spoon that is relatively long enough when dealing with man, because anything can happen, especially in terms of business or investment deals where money is involved. That is to say, in business or investment deals, you cannot be too careful with men. Therefore you must ensure that all the cards are placed on the table before you agree to play. You must ensure that all the loose ends are tied neatly; that all the t's are crossed and all the i's are dotted; that all the small prints (terms and conditions) are read, interpreted and understood before you sign the dotted line to close the deal. With this, it becomes quite difficult for anyone to take advantage of you or to defraud you.

Nevertheless, much as it is true that man is naturally depraved, and that majority of the human population is composed of the bad and the ugly, this does not exclude the fact that we also have the good in the human society.

This implies that though man is not an angel, man is also not a devil; he only has high tendency or propensity towards evil because of the Adamic (sinful) nature that he inherited. But beyond this, man is really an angel at heart, especially in his original, pure, Edenic or redeemed state. And the reason is not far-fetched – he was created in the image of the good God. This is why we have some good and very good people in the world, even though they are in the minority.

This brings us to why we must have some trust in man, at least until he proves himself otherwise. Of course, I am not advocating for absolute trust in man. But if you must have good relationships with men, then you must trust the people you relate with to some extent. This is more imperative in marital and business relationships. The subject of trust in marital relationship is reserved for another text or some other authors who are authorities in that field. Our concern here is that we must build as well as hazard some trust in our business relationships.

Honesty, Sincerity and Integrity

Honesty, sincerity and integrity are triplets that would lift anyone who possesses them to unimaginable heights of greatness. Honesty is the state of being honest (full of honour), just, fair in one's dealings, upright, free from fraud, candid, truthful, ingenuous, seemly, respectable, chaste and honourable. Integrity means entireness, wholeness, uprightness, honesty, purity and the unimpaired state of anything or any person. And sincerity is the state of being pure, unmixed, unadulterated, unfeigned, genuine, free from pretence, the same in reality as in appearance, truthful, etc.

We live in an age when humanity has turned truth upside down and inside out; and lies, half-truths and white lies are reigning sway. Today, the human society has embraced and is frolicking with Satan, the god of lies, deceit, falsehood and fraud. Today, more than ever before, people erroneously believe that you can make it to the extent of your ability to tell lies, deceive, cheat, steal and defraud. Man, today, has become a cat that cannot be entrusted with fish, and this is more evident in the attitude of man towards money.

Unfortunately, this terrible attitude of man is the reason why people are wary, scared and suspicious of their fellow men, especially as far as money is concerned. Today, men find it very difficult to trust their fellow men with their hard-earned money. This is because men all over the world have sold their souls to the devil and have made mammon (money) their god. Hence, today, men can do unimaginably dirty, wicked and dastard acts for filthy lucre's sake. Today, man's conscience has been seared with hot iron and is dead. Therefore, like the deaf and dumb dog, that he is, he rushes ahead without heeding the whistle of the hunter and plunges into the sea of the great inferno that awaits all liars, dishonest, insincere, fraudulent and greedily selfish people. And from there, he is to arise no more, through all eternity. This is the very sad and sordid state of today's human society.

Thus, today, the human society is in dire need of honest and sincere men who will hold the forte for truth and save humanity from destruction. The human society is eagerly looking for men of truth who will help rescue the world from the fangs of the dragon of lies, deceit and falsehood. And the man who dares to be sincere and walks by the truth is the man that will rule the world in this closing age of humanity.

And as far as the issues of money and wealth are concerned, men all over the world are looking for honest, sincere, truthful and trustworthy men and women into whose hands they can entrust their money for safe-keeping. And if you are such a man or woman of integrity, nothing and nobody in heaven, on earth or in hell can stop you from becoming a millionaire, a multi-millionaire, or even a billionaire. Really, honesty, sincerity and integrity are the best policies and they yield great rewards. And, as it has been said, if you lose your money, you have not lost anything; if you lose your health, you have lost something; but if you lose your integrity (character), you have lost everything. Integrity is all that you have. Strive to protect it, and it shall be well with you!

Thrift/Prudence

Chambers English Dictionary defines thrift in these several ways: the state of thriving, frugality, economy, prosperity, profitable occupation, increase in wealth, gain, savings, etc. These several definitions have a common decimal of financial increase or multiplication. Hence to be thrifty is to be prosperous or in good condition. And this prosperity is achieved through frugality or by being economical. The same Dictionary defines prudence as the quality of being cautious and wise in conduct, being discreet, behaviour that is dictated by forethought, etc. Prudence, as it relates to money, therefore, implies a handling of money in a wise, discreet and cautious manner. It refers to the habit of being careful with money or of handling money with wisdom and discretion.

The combination of prudence and thrift can lift any pauper and beggar to great and enviable wealth. These are the virtues that would enable him to spend wisely, discreetly and cautiously in order not to exceed the limit of his income. They are the virtues that would enable him to retain part of what he earns for the purpose of saving and investment. They are the virtues that are responsible for the accumulation of great wealth all over the world. They are the virtues that Joseph used to gather all the corn in the land of Egypt within the seven years of plenty. He was a man who was regarded as discreet and wise. And, even today, thrift and prudence are invaluable virtues for gathering wealth.

Nobody spends money to become rich. To be rich is to make money, save and invest some. Hence a rich man is not the one who makes and spends money, but he who retains some of his money for the purpose of wealth building. And to be rich, you must have the basic qualifications of thrift and prudence – you must be wise and discreet. When you have these invaluable qualities and you apply them correctly, the whole world will soon come knocking at your door to beg for provisions as they did to Joseph in Egypt. And it does not matter whether you are or have been in prison or dungeon of life or not. It is your thrift and prudence – wisdom and discretion – that will pull you out of the pit and out of the prison and lift you to the palace and unto the pinnacle of life. This is a faithful saying, and it is worthy of all acceptation!

Diligence

Proverbs 22:29 seems to say it all: "Seest thou a man diligent in his business? he shall stand before kings; he shall not stand before mean men." Diligence is required for standing out in life. Diligence is earnest application, industry or hard work. A diligent person is one who earnestly commits or immerses himself to or indulges in his work. A diligent person is a hard worker; he delights in dignity of labour.

As far as financial prosperity is concerned, there is no room for laziness. In fact, "He becometh poor that dealeth with a slack hand; but the hand of the diligent maketh rich." (Proverbs 10:4). So, diligence is what accounts for the difference between the rich and the poor. So much labour is required from any person who really wants to make it and become wealthy in life. Nobody gets rich or becomes wealthy on the bed of idleness, because there is no future for a lazy man. Slothfulness is one habit that the Bible strongly condemns without mincing words. Slothfulness is the fastest way to become a beggar:

> Go to the ant, thou sluggard; consider her ways, and be wise; which having no guide, overseer or ruler, provideth her meat in the summer, and gathereth her food in the harvest. How long wilt thou sleep, O sluggard? When wilt thou arise out of sleep? Yet a little sleep, a little slumber, a little folding of the hands to sleep; So shall thy poverty come as one that travelleth, and thy want as an armed man.

What comes to the lazy man is poverty and want. "He becometh poor that dealeth with a slack hand." Also, "the soul of the sluggard desireth, and hath nothing; but the soul of the diligent shall be made fat." (Proverb 13:4). So what comes to the diligent is wealth and abundance. "…he that gathereth by labour shall increase" (Proverbs 13:11). And particularly in business, profit comes through labour (Proverbs 14:23).

Therefore, if you desire to become a millionaire, go to work, and become very diligent at what you are doing; do whatever your hand finds to do with all your might, and "The Lord shall open unto thee his good treasure…to bless all the work of thine hand" (Deuteronomy 28:12). Just be diligent!

3

It's a Game of Numbers

Largely, the people who win in life are those who take life as a game. *Chambers English Dictionary* defines 'game', among other definitions, as (1) a contest for recreation; (2) a competitive amusement according to a system of rules; (3) the requisite number of points to be gained to win a game; (4) any object of pursuit; (5) scheme or method or method of seeking an end or the policy that would be most likely to attain it; (6) business, activity, operation; (7) fighting spirit; (8) gallantry; (9) having the spirit of a fighting cock; (10) plucky, courageous; and (11) having the necessary and willingness for some act. Some of these definitions are quite shocking, but they are all very revealing and interesting.

Life is a game; it is a contest for recreation. Until you see life as a contest, you will never win at it. See and approach life as a game you must win by all means. People who don't see life as such are never serious in life. They are the people who are so complacent and live their lives with nonchalance. Such people are never serious about whatever they are doing. They care less whether they succeed or make it or not. Such people are okay as long as they have food to eat, some clothes to wear and a place to perch. They have no visions, dreams or goals they are pursuing in life. They are not seeking to win any laurel; and they do not desire to make any impact anywhere. These are the people we can aptly describe as existing rather than living. Any well-meaning person who would make impact in life must see life as a contest that he must win at all costs. He must see it as a do or die affair; and he must be willing to give it all it takes.

But the person must know that he is not contesting against any other person; rather, that he is contesting against himself. Really, in the game of life, you have no opponent; you are your own opponent. Yes, you are not trying to outdo or surpass anybody. In other words, you are trying to exceed your best or to break your own records. The game becomes so interesting when you approach it this way. Nobody gets hurt in the process; and you surely emerge a winner, because you can always stretch beyond your elasticity limits if you try hard enough. And this is where the fun comes in.

Yes, life is a contest for recreation. You are not trying to win in this game so that people can clap for you. No! You are simply exercising yourself, and catching fun at it. You are just seeking to find out how much further you can go. You are checking and testing your inner, physical, mental and emotional strength. You are seeking to know how much impact you can make in life. And, when you discover that you are capable of going far beyond the best you have ever been, or the best you thought you can ever be, this alone gives you the kind of satisfaction that you can never find through any other way. And this satisfaction is what is called fulfillment, which cannot be quantified in any numerical or monetary value. It is what money cannot buy.

Life is also a competitive amusement according to a system of rules. What makes life competitive is not because you are struggling with anybody for anything. God has filled the world with great abundance. There is abundant provision for all. What makes life competitive is the fact that your own resources are limited, and many things are competing with your limited resources. You have limited time of 24 hours per day, seven days per week, 28, 29, 30 or 31 days per month, 365 or 366 days or 52 weeks or 12 months per year; and you are limited to only one life span of between 70 and 120 years on earth. Also, no matter how rich or wealthy you may be, you have limited amount of money. And, very importantly, you have limited opportunities at your disposal per time. Then, as I said earlier, very many things, people and issues are competing for these limited resources. This is why life is a competitive game.

But life is a game that is very amusing. So many things, people, places and issues are so amazingly wonderful, beautiful and interesting that you cannot but be excited and amused by them. And when you choose to focus on this sunny side of life, life becomes a source of joy and happiness to you. On the other hand, life is also filled with a lot of challenges, afflictions, troubles, trials and temptations. But when you focus on this dark side of life, life becomes drudgery and a misery. Not that anyone can avoid any of these, but one can choose to confront them with the right attitude. And the right attitude is to see the challenges as part of the game of life – that makes life more interesting and amusing.

Another thing about life is that it is a game that is played according to a system of rules. Every game has its rules; and life, being a game, has its own rules. The rules of the game of life are called laws of nature or principles of life. For anyone to live a happy, joyous and fulfilled life, he must obey the laws of nature or the principles of life. To go against them is to shoot oneself at the foot and to lose out in the game of life. Hence everyone who really desires to live a worthwhile, successful and prosperous life must seek to know the system of rules that guide the game of life. When these rules are found and accurately applied, life becomes very interesting, exciting and amusing.

'Game' is also defined as any object of pursuit. In this case, life becomes a vision or dream you must realize or a goal you must reach or score. And this is what makes the difference between an achiever and an underachiever; and between a fulfilled and an unfulfilled man. If you do not have any dream or vision you are pursuing in life, then life will be an aimless adventure for you. If you do not have any goal you want to reach in life, then life will be a mirage, and you will become a rolling stone that gathers no moss. Therefore, to make your life meaningful, you must see it as an object of pursuit; you must set a standard, a goal or a vision for yourself, which becomes the driving force for living your life. And this, among other factors, make your life interesting and worth living.

Life is a game; it is a scheme or method of seeking an end, or the policy that would most likely help to attain it.

This means that life is not an end in itself, but a means to an end. And to make the game of life interesting, you must know and establish the end that you have in mind. For some people, the end is to become fabulously wealthy; for others, it is to contribute immensely to humanity and make a great impact in society; and for yet others, it is to live for God and make heaven at last. Hence, what you live for is what determines the life you live. You must first determine your destination before you determine the route you will take to get there. Life is indeed the scheme, method or process you adopt for getting to your final destination – your promised land.

Life is a business, activity, operation. Until you begin to face life as a business, life will not work for you. The great mistake that very many of us are making is that we often separate our life from our business. And this is what is responsible for the high failure rate in the human society. Our life is our business, just as our business is our life. If you succeed in business and fail in life, you have failed; and if you succeed in life and fail in business, your success is incomplete, and you have failed in the true sense of it. You are a business entity, and you should approach life in a business-like way. And don't you ever forget this: your life is your business, and your business is your life. Therefore organize your life the same way you would organize your business firm. Keep proper and accurate records of your activities the same way you would keep the records of your business activities. Above all, become profit and result-oriented the same way you would in business. Life is indeed a business. Run it as such.

Another thing about life is that it is activity. Life is not a passive phenomenon; rather, it is action, or a series of actions (activities). Whatever has life has action or activity. Whatever has no action or activity has no life – it is dead. To prove that you are alive, you must be engaged in some activities; if not, you will be taken for a corpse, and you will indeed begin to stink. And, of course, you must watch the kind of activities you go into. Not all activities lead to progress. In fact, some activities lead to retrogression, while some result in stagnation. Therefore watch the kind of actions or activities you go into. But even at that, wrong action or activity is better than inaction or inactivity. At worse, you will gain experience from the wrong action or activity. But you have nothing to gain from inactivity more than your sense of failure or morbidity. So rise up, and do something, anything; but never stand or sit still like a statue.

Similarly, life is operation. And you are the operations manager of your life. No business operates without opening its doors for the world to know. Very many of us are hanging the 'Closed' sign on our lives. Hence nothing significant is happening in and around us. But you must immediately wake up and hang up the 'Now Opened' sign for the world around you to know that you are still in operation. And there is nobody who will do it for you. You are the sole operator of your life. Your life stops when you stop operation, and your life reverberates into motion and accelerates when you turn on the ignition key of your life. Go into operation and make your life productive, and the world will patronize, and even celebrate you at last.

Life is a game that requires the fighting spirit. Winning, in virtually every game in life, is never easy to come by. In fact, we have more quitters in virtually every game than winners. To emerge a winner in any game, you need very strong determination to keep on keeping on till you win. You need the die-hard or never-say-die spirit to keep at it to the end. This is what is called the fighting spirit. You need to have it because nothing good comes easy. In life, nobody gets anything on a platter of gold. Everybody must fight to get what he wants. To give up at any time is to lose out and never to have what you desire in life. But to hold on and hold out is to take the chance of winning and receiving the laurels that you want in life.

And as far as the issue of becoming a millionaire is concerned, nobody becomes one without a fighting spirit. Authorities and experts have established that over 80% of the world's millionaires arose from poor lower class families. What is responsible for this is that these people have a very strong fighting spirit – that is responsible for propelling them and lifting them out of the dungeon of poverty to the realm of great wealth. Thus the fighting spirit is an indispensable requirement for wealth building. It is this spirit that will enable you to work and keep working, strive and keep striving, give and keep giving, save and keep saving, invest and keep investing, pray and keep praying, believe and keep believing until you arrive at great wealth, and until you move from a nonentity to a celebrity in life.

Life is all about gallantry. No timid, chicken-hearted person goes to the warfront and comes back alive. Only gallant soldiers are allowed to go to the warfront. Life is a battlefield, and the battle, most often, is very fierce; and it takes gallantry to pull through and survive the battles of life. The battle is even fiercer in the issues of wealth and wealth accumulation. It is in fact one of the hottest warfronts. It is so hot that millions have ended up as casualties in the course of battling for money. This is why you must have all it takes to fight and emerge a winner in this game; I mean this battle. And one major requirement is gallantry; that is, bravery or intrepidity. Without it, no soldier ventures into and survives any battle, let alone win victory in it. Do you have it? Think about it!

An image that aptly depicts the right attitude to the game of life is, having the spirit of a fighting cock. Have you ever seen or witnessed the scene of two fighting cocks? They are always red with rage and with strong determination to defeat the other. The feathers on their neck, wings and tail are always ruffled and stand out in awe. Their wings, claws and beaks are always drawn for the fight; and they fly and swoop against each other with unbelievable belligerence and agility. This is the kind of spirit that is needed for winning in the game of life. You must approach life with the spirit of a fighting cock. You must go into the battle of life with the attitude of 'No Retreat, No Surrender'. This is the attitude that emerges victorious, particularly in the battle for wealth. It is a fight to finish.

I remember when I was a little boy playing on the sand with my peers in the village. Whenever we saw two cocks fighting, we would plant a broom stick standing upright on the ground, with the belief that as long as the broom stick remains standing, the two cocks will fight and keep fighting until one of them or both of them drop dead. We believed that the broom stick would mysteriously instill in the two fighting cocks the strong determination to fight to finish – never to give up. I wonder where that belief came from. It is a strange one indeed. Anyway, we never ever saw any cock drop dead; we never had the patience to wait for that to happen; after some minutes, we often would kick down or pluck up the broom stick and chase the fighting cocks away. But the lesson I learnt from that is, man and life are like fighting cocks; and man must not stop fighting until he wins the fight or until he drops dead. This is the spirit of the fighting cock; it is the spirit that is needed by any man who would win in the game of life and in the battle for wealth. It is the spirit of a fighting cock.

Another attitude that is needed in the game of life is the plucky, courageous, pertinacious, obstinate and unyielding spirit. He who gives up too soon and so easily can never become a winner in the game of life. There is something about life that demands persistence from man before it yields to him. It seems that life delights in testing the tenacity of man before it yields to his demands. It seems that life wants to find out how resolute man is about what he wants before life makes a way for him to get it.

In my first book, *A to Z of Success Secrets*, I referred to the terminology that Sunny Obazu-Ojeagbase uses to describe tenacity. He calls it 'the goat mentality'. This is the spirit that never gives up. This is the obstinate, stubborn, unyielding spirit that keeps the goat coming again and again for the object of its heart's desire, no matter how many times you try to stop it. This is the spirit that any man who wants to become a millionaire must have. He must have the plucky, courageous, pertinacious, obstinate, stubborn and unyielding spirit that will enable him to keep trying, to keep working, to keep saving, and to keep investing, again and again and again until he becomes a millionaire and a multimillionaire that the world will celebrate. This is the spirit of a winner. Go for it.

The last definition we are examining, about life being a game, is that of having the necessary willingness for some act. Nobody wins any game by standing or sitting still. In every game, you have to do something to win at it. So there are some necessary acts to go into to win the game. A football team, for instance, that is not ready to go for the attack is not ready to score any goal and cannot win the match. And if the same team is not bothered about defending its goal post against the opponent's assaults, then that football team should get ready to lose the match. It is the same with the game of life. There are necessary things to do to win at the game of life. And anyone who is not ready to do what is required should get ready to lose in life.

And in doing what is required for winning in life, there must be willingness. This is because you are your own coach, technical adviser or manager in the game of life. Everybody has his own life to live. Therefore you should not expect anybody to leave his own life to come and help you to live your life. In the game of life, you are on your own. You must know what is required, and you must be willing and ready to do what is required at the right time and in the right way. What this means is that you are your own prompter; you are your own cheerleader; you are your own time-keeper; you are your own quality controller. To wait for anybody to do these for you is to wait forever and to fail in the game of life. Therefore, whatever you need to do to win in the game of life, stand up and start doing it right now, and be sure to do it very well and on time. And if becoming a millionaire is one game that you desire to win in life, then you must know what is required for becoming a millionaire, and you must rise up and start doing them right now and in the right way.

Life Is a Game of Numbers

Life is a game of numbers. Virtually in every game of life, numbers are the indicators for both winners and losers. Often, the person(s) with the highest number become(s) the winner(s). Hence, to be a winner at the game of life, you must be comfortable with numbers. And this is where I made a big mistake in my early school days. I was not comfortable with numbers; in fact, I hated numbers (figures) with a passion, and I did everything humanly possible to avoid coming in contact with numbers. Hence, in those days, my arithmetic/mathematics teachers would come into the classroom with one door, and I would go out through the other door. I had so much hatred for numbers and all those mathematical symbols, equations and calculations. Therefore when it was time to choose subjects and make career choice, I did not think twice, I dropped all the subjects that have anything to do with calculations and went for the art-related subjects. And this is why I ended up with B.A. (Hons) English, M.A. English and Ph.D. Linguistics. But later in life, especially when I went to do an MBA, I was to learn that the game of life is really about numbers, and that nobody can successfully run away from numbers; else he will fail in the game of life.

Life is a game of numbers, and man is a victim of numbers. He was created on a particular numbered day; conceived in the womb out of a particular numbered sperms; born after a particular numbered months and on a particular numbered day; weaned after a particular numbered days; dedicated after a particular numbered months; went to school for particular numbered years; had his results calculated with numbers and came out with a particular numbered position or grade; got married on a particular numbered date; had a number of children and particular number of sexes, all born on particular numbered dates; must work for a particular number of years and retire after a particular number of years and must die after a particular number of years and on a particular numbered date. So it is clear that man is really a victim of numbers, for no man can really escape from numbers.

Even the human society in which we live is driven by numbers. And there is no part of the society that is more affected or influenced by numbers than the economy. All the indices of a society's economy are determined and indicated by numbers. And much more importantly, money which could be described as the oil or fuel that lubricates and runs the economy, works through numbers. In fact, we can say that there is no money without numbers. The reason is that money is not composed of the currency notes and coins that we spend in the society; money is not the paper currency or cheques. Rather, money is the value allocated to those currency notes and cheques and coins that are used for exchange of goods and services. And value is quantified in numbers. So a millionaire or billionaire or even a trillionaire is not known by the quality or quantity of the paper money or gold coins that he carries about, but by the great value of his assets; that is, his net worth. And for any man to know, appreciate and competently manage his net worth, he must be comfortable with numbers and learn how they work in monetary terms. Thus, working with money is, indeed, playing the game of numbers.

All the economic or business transactions that are done in the world are carried out with money or monetary equivalents that are quantified in numbers or that have numerical values. Even the Stock Exchange operates with numbers. Therefore anybody who is deficient in the knowledge of numbers has placed himself at a disadvantaged position in the game of life and in the business and economic world. So, regardless of your field of endeavour, you must rise up and begin to acquire the knowledge of numbers so you can fit into the world of commerce and finance that rule the world's economies.

Becoming a Millionaire Is a Game of Numbers

Seriously speaking, becoming a millionaire is a game of numbers. A millionaire is simply a person who has accumulated a monetary net worth of up to seven digits of any country's currency, such as N1,000,000 or $1,000,000 or £1,000,000 or €1,000,000. What this means is that the moment a person has acquired or accumulated the first one million of the country's currency, that person is qualified to be called a millionaire.

And being able to earn, acquire, gather or accumulate one million of a person's currency is what the war about becoming a millionaire is all about. In the first chapter of this book, we said and agreed that any fool can become a millionaire. But that is the ideal situation. The real fact of life is that about 90-95% of the world's population, from the ages past to the present have not been able to achieve this feat, as simple as it seems. A large majority of the people in the world have ended up far below the millionaire target. And this is rather unfortunate and both disheartening and very discouraging.

So, the question that readily and perpetually hangs on every lip is, is it so difficult to become a millionaire? And the answer to this is, NO! Becoming a millionaire is not as difficult as it seems. It is a matter of understanding that it is a game of numbers. It is as simple as knowing the first number with which you begin to count up to 1,000,000. And the first number, as you can see here, is 1. What this means is that once you begin to count from 1 and you do not stop counting, you are sure to get to 1,000,000. And beginning to count is to earn, acquire and set aside the first coin or currency note in your journey towards becoming a millionaire. For, as has been strongly said by Robert Schuller, beginning is half done; which means that once you have taken the first step towards becoming a millionaire, the others will naturally follow.

The sole reason why many people have not achieved the feat of becoming millionaires is because they have not taken the first step. To them, the dream of becoming a millionaire is so lofty and the journey so scary that they dare not venture in that direction. But this is just an unfounded fear; it is both falsehood and a fallacy. Becoming a millionaire is not as lofty, difficult and scary as that. All that you have to do is to face your fears and eat that frog, as Brian Tracy would say. All that you have to do is to reduce or belittle the mountain and climb it from the bottom up.

Begin at the Flat End

As a Nigerian (Yoruba) proverb has it, to eat solid pap, you have to begin at the flat end. It is the same with becoming a millionaire; you have to begin at the flat end. And what is the flat end of becoming a millionaire? The flat end is to try to accumulate a million kobo, pesewa, cents, or shillings. Question: How much is one million kobo? Answer: Ten thousand naira.

i.e. $1,000,000k \div 100 = N10,000$

Next question: How long will it take you to accumulate N10,000? Answer: It depends on your earning ability and saving capacity. But assuming you are earning low, and you are able to save only N10 per day, then it will take you 1,000 days to accumulate N10,000, which is equivalent to 2 years and seven months. And if you save N10,000 every 1,000 days or 2.7years, then it means that to save N1,000,000, you will need about 274 years. Of course you know that nobody lives that long. Therefore to realize your dream of becoming a millionaire in your life time you have to find a way to increase your earning capacity and saving ability. And if you can save just N27 per day, it means you will save N10,000 in 370 days; that is, approximately one year. If you are able to save N10,000 every year, it also means that you will need 100 years to save N1,000,000. And you also know that just a few people live up to 100 years today. So, what do you do? Find a way to earn more and increase your saving capacity. And if you are able to earn more and increase your saving to, say, N55 per day, then you will save N10,000 in 182 days, which means that you will save N20,000 in one year. And if you save N20,000 every year, it means you will need about 50 years to accumulate N1,000,000. Can you believe that? Anybody who can save just N55 per day can become a millionaire in 50 years! So, nobody is supposed to die poor! But why are people not becoming millionaires? We shall talk about that later.

For now, let us see if we can increase our income a little more and commit to saving N100 per day. If anybody is able to do this, that person will accumulate a million naira in 27 years. Now, increase your saving by 100% (i.e. N200) per day and you will need only thirteen and half years to become a millionaire. And if you are daring enough to increase your saving per day to N500, it means you will need only five and half years to become a millionaire. Better still, if you can be disciplined enough to suspend all self-gratification and commit to saving N1,000 per day (what some people spend at eateries on a plate of food or at a drinking bar per day), then in a little above two and half years, you will become a millionaire! Now, do you see how simple it is to become a millionaire? So, can anything or anyone stop you from becoming one now? The ball is in your court!

20 Ways to Accumulate One Million Naira

1. N1,000,000 at N1 per day = 2,740 years
2. N1,000,000 at N5 per day = 548 years
3. N1,000,000 at N10 per day = 274 years
4. N1,000,000 at N25 per day = 109 years
5. N1,000,000 at N50 per day = 55 years
6. N1,000,000 at N75 per day = 36 years
7. N1,000,000 at N100 per day = 27 years
8. N1,000,000 at N150 per day = 18 years
9. N1,000,000 at N200 per day = 13.5 years
10. N1,000,000 at N250 per day = 11 years
11. N1,000,000 at N300 per day = 9 years
12. N1,000,000 at N400 per day = 7 years
13. N1,000,000 at N500 per day = 5.5 years
14. N1,000,000 at N750 per day = 3.5 years
15. N1,000,000 at N1,000 per day = 2.7 years
16. N1,000,000 at N1,500 per day = 1.8 years
17. N1,000,000 at N2,000 per day = 1.4 years
18. N1,000,000 at N2,750 per day = 1 year
19. N1,000,000 at N3,500 per day = 7 months
20. N1,000,000 at N5,500 per day = 5 months

The above table shows that it is quite simple to become a millionaire. All you need to do is to choose any of the above plans that fits into your earning capacity and start, never to stop saving until you become a millionaire.

But do you know that the above table does not reflect the truth about how long it will take to become a millionaire at the various given savings amounts per day? The truth is that it will take far less than those various time frames to become a millionaire with the given amounts. What would be responsible for the reduction of the time frame is the miracle of compound interest. If a man saves, for instance, N200 per day, he would save N73,000 in one year. If he invests that money in an average yielding investment of, say, 20% interest per annum, then he will earn an interest of N14,600 in the first year; which means his money will appreciate to N87,600 at the end of the second year. When you add this amount to the N73,000 that he will save that second year, it means he will have N160,000 that is ready to be invested against the third year. When he does invest this amount, he will earn an interest of N32,120, which brings the money up to N192,720. And when his N73,000 saving of the third year is added to it, he would have the sum of N265,720 that he would invest against the forth year, and which will earn him an interest of N53,144. This interest plus his capital plus savings of the forth year will bring his money up to N391,864. When this money is invested against the fifth year, it will earn him N78,373 which makes his money appreciate to N470,237. This, plus his savings of the fifth year, gives him N543,237 that is to be invested against the sixth year, where he will earn an interest of N108,647. At the end of the sixth year, his capital plus his interest plus his year's savings will amount to N724,884. When this is invested in the seventh year, he earns N144,977. Hence his total holding at the end of the seventh year will be N724,884 plus N144,977 plus N73,000 equals N942,861. When this amount is invested in the eighth year, he earns an interest of N188,572, which when added to his capital and his eighth year's savings will give him N1,204,433. Which means that rather than become a millionaire in thirteen and half years at N200 per day, the man will end up as a millionaire in just 8 years. This is the miracle of compound interest!

In the same way, a man who saves N500 per day will have N182,500 At the end of the first year. If he invests this money in a 20% interest yielding business, he will earn N45,625 which brings his money up to N228,125 plus N182,500 equals N410,625 at the end of the second year. When this money is invested in the third year, he earns N102,656 plus his capital plus his third year savings equals N695,781. When he invests this amount in the fourth year, he will earn N173,945 which brings his money to N695,781 plus N173,945 plus N182,500 equals N1,043,671. This means that this man who saves N500 per day will become a millionaire in four years instead of five and half years.

The two examples that we have discussed above are clearly presented in the two tables below:

S/N	Yr	D/S N	T/S N	Invest. N	20% Interest N	Total Holding N
1.	1st Yr	200	73,000	–	–	73,000
2.	2nd Yr	200	73,000	73,000	14,600	160,600
3.	3rd Yr	200	73,000	160,000	32,120	265,720
4.	4th Yr	200	73,000	265,720	53,144	470,237
5.	5th Yr	200	73,000	470,237	78,373	543,237
6.	6th Yr	200	73,000	543,237	108,647	724,884
7.	7th Yr	200	73,000	724,884	144,977	942,861
8.	8th Yr	200	73,000	942,861	188,572	1,204,433
			Total	**584,000**		**1,204,433**

S/N	Yr	D/S N	T/S N	Amt Invest N	25% Interest N	Total Holding N
1.	1st Yr	500	182,500	—	—	182,500
2.	2nd Yr	500	182,500	182,500	45,625	410,625
3.	3rd Yr	500	182,500	410,625	102,656	695,781
4.	4th Yr	500	182,500	695,781	173,945	1,043,671
	Total		730,000			1,043,671

So you can see that life is a game of numbers; and becoming a millionaire is just a game of numbers. But it is a game that you must be willing to play. Nobody wins a game that he is not involved in, no matter how much interest he has in the game. Majority of people in the world are mere spectators in the millionaires' game. They are only watching the very few people who are playing the game. Some are so intrigued by the game that they have joined the fans club to clap hands for and cheer up those who are playing the game. Some others have even graduated to become financial, investment or economic analysts for the millionaires' game. But the sad thing is that these very enthusiastic spectators, fans and analysts are not involved in playing the game, hence they remain poor, year in year out, while those who are playing the game are growing richer and richer every day. And this is really very sad

The only way to become a millionaire is to get involved in playing the millionaires' game. It is the game of making money; it is the game of saving money; it is the game of investing money; it is the game of making your money to work for you; and above all, it is the game of numbers, which showcases the miracle of compound interest. Get involved in this game; it works wonders!

4

4 Most Essential Knowledge in Life

We all need knowledge to function effectively in life. And the four most important areas of knowledge that everybody must seek to acquire in order to function well in life are:
- The knowledge of God
- The knowledge of man
- The knowledge of the world
- The knowledge of money

Let us examine briefly why these four areas of knowledge are regarded as the most important and identify where they could be acquired.

A. The Knowledge of God

God is the Creator of the universe, including man. In fact, God made man in His own image, and even breathed into man's nostrils for him to become a living soul. In other words, without God, man cannot exist. No wonder, God's word says, it is in Him (God) that we live, move and have our being. Thus man's existence is totally dependent on God.

Man is the image, the reflection of God. Therefore for man to know himself, he must first seek to know God, the original copy. That is to say, you can never know yourself in the true sense of it if you do not know God. And if you don't know yourself, you can never function effectively in life. Hence, your optimal performance, satisfaction and fulfillment in life are totally dependent on your knowledge of God.

Fortunately for us, God has not hidden the knowledge about himself from man. The manual that thoroughly exposes the knowledge of God to man is the Holy Bible; and the institution that helps to interpret the manual and that teaches the knowledge of God to people is the Church. What this means is that if you have a copy of the Holy Bible and you join a good Bible teaching Church, then you have access to the knowledge of God, the first of the four most important areas of knowledge in life. To refuse to have and read a copy of the Bible, and to refuse to join a good Bible teaching Church, is to deny yourself access to the knowledge of Him whose image you are; it is, consequently, to deny yourself access to the knowledge of who you are. For, you can know yourself and function better when you know God in whose image you were created.

B. The Knowledge of Man

What we have just said above leads us to the need for man to seek to know himself. It takes us to the age-old admonition, "Man, know thyself." The need for man to know himself is so important, particularly in this age when man has done practically everything possible to abuse himself. No wonder it has been said that when the purpose of a thing is unknown, abuse is inevitable. Man has continued to grossly abuse himself and his fellow man because he does not really know himself and the purpose of his existence. If only man can seek to know himself and his purpose better, much of the unmitigated atrocities being perpetrated by man in the human society would be non-existent; the society would have been a paradise of bliss. But we all know, unfortunately, that the reverse is the case. Therefore we all need to seek for and acquire the knowledge of man.

Fortunately for us too, there is a place that is designated for acquiring the knowledge of man – the school. Anyone who is privileged to go to school is privileged to learn more about man than the person who did not go to school. It is at school that we have the privilege of reading books and are taught the various subjects that expose the nature and composition of man. This knowledge enables us to know man better, as well as enables us to bring out the best in us for the purpose of performing optimally in life.

C. The Knowledge of the World

Another area of knowledge that we have the privilege of acquiring is the world around us. The world is the natural habitat where man operates. And for man to operate effectively, he must have relative knowledge of the world around him. All of the scientific and technological wonders that we are experiencing in the world today are testimonies to the extent to which man has been able to understand his natural and material environment, and how far and how well he has been able to convert these to useful materials to make life much easier for him.

Hence, the more man learns about his world, the more he understands it and the more he manipulates it for his convenience and enjoyment. This is why every man must seek to acquire the knowledge of the world around him. Failure to do this will make man a blind and ignorant sojourner who stumbles about the rough terrains of life, and is in danger of falling into the dark bottomless pit of dissatisfaction and endless regrets.

And as I hinted earlier, the school is the designated institution where we learn much about the world around us. And that is why educated people have the greater propensity to better appreciate and organize the human, natural and material resources around them.

So far in this section, we have identified three of the four most important areas of knowledge:

- God
- Man
- The World

We have also identified the designated institutions where these three areas of knowledge are taught or could be acquired respectively:

- God – at the Church
- Man – at School
- The World – at School

But we must at this point emphasize that any man who is able to acquire these three most important areas of knowledge is better equipped to function more effectively than anyone who is ignorant regarding these three knowledge bases. But we must also strongly point out that the man who acquires these three important areas of knowledge is not fully equipped to function optimally until he acquires the fourth of the most important areas of knowledge - Money.

D. The Knowledge of Money

Whether anybody knows it or not, money is the oil that lubricates the world (the human society) in which man operates. Hence, if you have the knowledge of God, the Creator of the world and of man who lives in it; if you have the knowledge of man, the operator (or manager) of the world; if you have the knowledge of the world, the resources around the world; and you lack the knowledge of money, the oil (or fluid) that enables the resources to flow freely, you will most likely have great difficulties in getting things organized to achieve your desired goals or to realize your desired dreams. Hence, with all your getting, get understanding or the knowledge of money in order to make things work for you.

So, if you want to get the knowledge of money, where do you go to acquire it? Well, your guess is as good as mine: Nowhere! What? Can't I get it at the Church? I don't think so; if not, all Christians or Church goers would have been great handlers of money. But you and I know very well that the reverse is actually the case. What about the school? Of course, they teach next to nothing about money at school; this is why most educated people are financial illiterates in the true sense of the word. In that case, the financial institutions should be our best bet. But, alas! This is not the case either. If so, many of us who visit and patronize the financial institutions would have been financial or economic wizards and multi-millionaires by now. But, on the contrary, the financial institutions always succeed in taking advantage of our financial ignorance to further impoverish us. So, as you can see, we have nowhere to turn to for this very important knowledge, and we are more or less helpless.

What we are really saying here is that we have a faulty education system in which nobody taught or teaches you about money. Yet, understanding money – what it is, how it works, how to make it work for you, how to earn it, and how to keep it – is absolutely essential to your life, your relationships, your world, your happiness and your future. To exclude the knowledge of money from your education is to exclude you from the best that life has to offer. Above all, learning how to become financially successful is one of the most critical skills that you must seek to acquire.

And as we said earlier, money skill is not taught at school or at any other designated institution in the world. Therefore, everyone must bear his own burden here. Fortunately for us, in addition to the Holy Bible that has some exposure on money, many self help books have been written by men who have learnt from experience and by the rule of thumb (in fact many of them, including me, got their fingers burnt in the process). It therefore behooves a man of wisdom to seek out the Bible and some of such books on money (including this one), and seek out a quiet place, to read, learn and acquire the knowledge of money, the fourth of the most important areas of knowledge that man needs to have in order to perform optimally in life.

5

What You Must Know about Money

Before we talk about what money is, it is necessary that we first correct our erroneous view about money. In other words, we need to first understand what money is not. If you put your hand into your pocket or purse right now, you would probably feel or come out with some crispy currency notes of various denominations or some coins of varying amounts. With these, you could easily pass as one who has money. But can we really call these pieces of paper or pieces of metal money? Well, sorry to disappoint you, money is not the piece of metal or paper that you give or that is given to you in exchange for goods and services. The piece of metal or paper is simply a promissory note or a legal tender that is given in lieu of the value that is placed on what is being exchanged for it. The piece of metal or paper does not hold value on its own. It is only valuable for as long as the law allows it to be used for exchange of goods and services.

I remember, before the early seventies, we were using the pounds and shillings in Nigeria until Naira and Kobo were introduced as legal tender to replace the pounds and shillings. Thenceforth, the pounds and shillings ceased to be acceptable as legal tenders. Some of our parents and grandparents probably kept samples of the Nigerian pounds and shillings to show to their children, grandchildren and great-grandchildren. Now, if any of our parents or grandparents should bring out some of those pounds and shillings today and give them to us, can we go to the market or superstore and use them to buy things? No? Why not? But they are still pounds and shillings! And they still carry the imprints, superscriptions and colours that have been on them! Can you now see why we cannot regard such or similar pieces of paper or metal as money? They do not hold value by themselves. Rather, value is conferred on them by the law that allows them to be used as means of exchange; and the moment the same law disallows their use as media of exchange, they automatically lose value.

Another thing about the pieces of paper and metal that we use as medium of exchange is that the value on them is not stable. The value fluctuates in relation to market forces. But the money that is regarded as real money has more stability in value. You will soon see that.

What Then Is Money?

I remember, in our Economics class in those days, we were taught that money is a medium of exchange. Of course this is a good definition of money. But it is an inexhaustive definition; it takes us back to the piece of metal or paper that is given as a medium of exchange.

In that our Economics class, we were also taught that money is what money can buy; that is to say, money is what you buy with the coin or currency note that you give in exchange for it. This definition really takes the status of money from the coin or currency note and gives it to something else. This definition implies that if I give out a N1,000 note to a seller and I receive in return a pair of trousers, the money is not the N1, 000 note that I gave out; rather, it is what I received in return. Does this therefore mean that the pair of trousers that I received in return is the money? And, the answer is, "No", because you may not always receive a pair of trousers in return whenever you give out a N1,000 note; you may receive something else in return. But the fact remains that every time you give out any amount of coin or currency note, you will always receive in return something that is valuable to you; and the more value you ascribe to what you receive in return, the more amount of coins or currency notes that you are willing to give in exchange for it.

So, money, in the real sense, is the value received. In this light, Brian Sher defines money simply as "a currency for trading value or benefits." Hence, the rich man is not he who has more coins or currency notes in his pocket or in his bank account, but he who receives more value for his money. If, for instance, Mr. A and Mr. B have N3 million each, and both of them desire to buy a Toyota Camry car; if Mr. A goes to the car shop and buys a brand new Toyota Camry car for N1.5 million, and Mr. B goes to the car shop and buys a similar brand new Toyota Camry car for N3 million, who can we say is the richer of the two buyers. Obviously, the richer person is the one who has more value for his money. Mr. B has spent all his money for one car, whereas Mr. A buys the same brand of car for half of the amount and still has half of his money left. In fact, Mr. A can use his N3 million to buy two brand new Camry cars or he can put the remaining N1.5 million in high-yielding investments that could give him more money. So, being rich is not having more money, but having more value for your money.

Another thing about money is that, it is not how much you earn that matters, but how much you are worth per time. This is what accounts for why two people could work at the same place and earn the same salary; but one may end up rich while the other may end up poor. Obviously, the one who ends up rich is the one who consumes less than he earns and saves and invests the surplus over time; while the one who ends up poor is the one who spends or consumes above his income and does not save or invest. So, really, it is not what you earn that determines your level of wealth per time; it is what you are able to consistently and persistently conserve, save and invest from what you earn.

And, at any point in time, everyone should be able to ascertain his level of wealth. In other words, every man should know his net worth per time. In *The Millionaire Next Door,* Thomas J. Stanley and William D. Danko have given us a simple rule of thumb or a formular for calculating one's expected net worth:

> Multiply your age by your realized pretax annual household income from all sources except inheritances. Divide by ten. This, less any inherited wealth, is what your net worth should be (13).

Mathematically, this is realized as:

$$\frac{\text{Age} \times \text{Annual Income}}{10}$$

So, assuming you are 40 years old, and your current monthly income is N80, 000, then your expected net worth is calculated as follows:

$$\text{Expected Net Worth} = \frac{\text{Age} \times \text{Annual Income}}{10}$$

$$= \frac{40 \times (80, 000 \times 12)}{10}$$

$$= \frac{40 \times 960, 000}{10}$$

$$= \frac{38,400, 000}{10}$$

$$= N3, 840, 000$$

What this means is that this 40 years old man whose annual income is N960, 000 is supposed to have accumulated a net worth of N3, 840, 000 by now; that is, if he is to retire financially independent. According to Stanley and Danko, if the actual net worth of the person is less than half of his expected net worth, then he is regarded as an Under Accumulator of Wealth (UAW); if his actual net worth is approximately equal to his expected net worth, he is an Average Accumulator of Wealth (AAW); and if his actual net worth is higher than double of his expected net worth, then he is regarded as a Prodigious Accumulator of Wealth (PAW). Stanley and Danko strongly hold and advocate that, for anyone to retire comfortably financially independent, he needs to aspire to be a P0 rodigious Accumulator of Wealth (PAW). What this translates into, in clear terms, is that if our 40 years old friend evaluated above is to retire comfortably financially independent, then he must aspire to double his net worth to at least N7, 680, 000 from his annual income of N960, 000. This appears to be an enormous task. But it is a realistic and possible task, especially with determination.

Therefore if you desire to retire comfortable and financially independent, you must immediately sit down and compute your expected net worth and compare it with your actual net worth. You will then discover whether you are an Under Accumulator of Wealth (UAW), an Average Accumulator of Wealth (AAW) or a Prodigious Accumulator of Wealth (PAW). If you discover that you are an Under Accumulator of Wealth, then it means you are going to retire poor and dependent on others at old age, unless you immediately do something drastic about remedying the situation. And that means you must immediately and drastically reduce your consumption rate in order to save and invest towards your future/retirement. If you discover that you are an Average Accumulator of Wealth (AAW), it means you will barely be comfortable and semi-independent at retirement, and you must also do something to improve on the situation. That is, you must further reduce your consumption rate to increase your savings, your investments and your net worth a little more to make for comfortable and financially independent retirement. If, however, you discover that you are a Prodigious Accumulator of Wealth (PAW), it means you have adequately prepared for a retirement of very comfortable financial independence, and I congratulate you. But this does not mean that you should rest on your oars. You can still do better than that. You can still keep on increasing your net worth, especially for the purpose of being a blessing and bequeathing a large estate to your beneficiaries and other members of the human society before and after your death. And the more people your wealth is able to bless or impact, and the farther it spreads into future generations, the better for you. So, striving to become a great Prodigious Accumulator of Wealth (PAW) is a very worthy pursuit that will bring joy to you both here and in eternity. Go for it!

6

How to Rise Above the Poverty Line

The international monetary community has established a thin line that demarcates between the poor and the rich. It is called, The Poverty Line, which is defined by one dollar a day. What this means is that, anyone who is earning and living below one dollar a day is internationally regarded as a very poor person. This also means that a person is wealthy to the level that he is able to rise above the poverty line. In this connection, the international monetary community has observed that, unfortunately, majority of people in the world are living below the poverty line; hence majority of people on earth are poor, and are living in acute poverty.

What has just been said above is not the complete story. The true story is that people are poor not only because they earn and live below the poverty line; rather, a large majority of people are poor because they conserve nothing for the purposes of investment and wealth building. Many of these people earn and live well above the poverty line but still remain poor. For instance, virtually all middle level income earners earn and live above one dollar a day, yet very many of them are very poor. Even, most business people, including petty traders make profits and live above the dollar a day, yet many of them are very poor. So, what is responsible for people being very poor is not really because they earn and live below the poverty line; rather, it is because they spend or consume all that they earn. And this is the true story of majority of people living on the planet earth today.

The unalloyed truth is that you can become wealthy to the level that you are able to earn and save above the poverty line. This means that until you are able to save and invest at least one dollar a day from your earnings, your struggle with poverty continues. You must therefore resolve to join the minority of people who are able to rise above the poverty line to become wealthy. And it begins with your having the determination to save a minimum of one dollar a day – every day – for the rest of your life.

Importance of Saving

So, rising above the poverty line begins with earning and saving above the dollar or its equivalents. It requires you to form the habit of saving consistently and persistently. It requires you to make a rock-solid decision to save a part of the money that enters your hand. It requires you to know that any money that comes to you has two divisions, each serving a specific purpose.

Two Divisions of Money (Income)

Any money (income) that comes to you is broadly divided into two parts:

- The Seed

- The Bread

And both the seed and the bread make up the fruit.

Whenever God gives you money, He is giving you a fruit that has both seed and bread, as shown in the scriptures below:

> For as the rain cometh down, and the snow from heaven, and returneth not thither, but watereth the earth, and maketh it bring forth and bud, that it may give seed to the sower, and bread to the eater. (Isaiah 55:10).

> Now he that ministered seed to the sower both minister bread for food, and multiply your seed sown, and increase the fruits of your righteousness. (2 Cor. 9:10).

As contained in Isaiah 55:10 above, the seed is for sowing, while the bread is for eating. Thus, whenever you eat both the seed and the bread of your income, you sign a pact with poverty, lack and want. It means you sacrifice your future on the altar of present gratification. This is because it is the seed that you sow today that will produce the bread that you will eat tomorrow. In fact, the seed you sow today guarantees your tomorrow's bread and future seeds. So, if you do not set aside any seed for sowing today, be very sure, you will not have bread to eat and seeds to sow tomorrow. The choice is yours. Choose to reserve seeds for sowing today so that you can have bread to eat and more seeds to sow tomorrow.

Any money that comes to you is first and foremost a seed, just as every grain of rice or corn or every tuber of yam is a seed. You can sow it and it can produce many more fruits that will give much more bread and uncountable seeds. You can also eat all and never have food to eat again.

Now, in some fruits, you can easily differentiate between the seed and the bread, e.g. mango, apple, pawpaw, orange, pear, etc. In such fruits, only the bread is edible, the seeds are not edible. So the tendency of mistakenly eating the seeds along with the bread does not arise, except in rare exceptional cases when you inadvertently swallow a seed in the course of eating the bread. In some cases, both the seeds and the bread are edible, even though they look different, e.g. guava, garden egg, cucumber, etc. In some other fruits, there is no remarkable designation or clear demarcation between the bread part and the seed part. The whole fruit looks the same through and through. For instance, which part of a tuber of yam is the seed and which part is the bread? Or, again, which part of groundnut, corn, rice, bean, etc is the seed and which part is bread? Hence, while it is very easy to eat the bread and reserve the seeds of such fruits as mango, pawpaw, pear, etc for sowing, it is not very easy to spare the seeds of such fruits as guava, garden egg, cucumber, groundnut, corn, bean, rice, etc for sowing. In most cases, the eater goes ahead to eat both the bread and the seeds together.

And this is the crime that is being committed by most people as far as money is concerned. For the obvious reason of absence of a clear demarcation between the bread part and the seed part, majority of us in the human society goes ahead to eat both our bread and our seeds, and thereby eat up our future. Hence we remain poor year in and year out. But we must make it very clear that rich people eat their bread and sow their seeds; and that is why they are rich. But poor people eat both their bread and their seed, and that is why they are poor, remain poor and even grow poorer. It is as the saying goes; you can't eat your cake and have it.

2 Ways Not to Become Rich

Try hard as you can, there are two ways you may choose to follow and you can never become rich:

1. Nobody spends money to become rich; and
2. Nobody hoards money to become rich.

Let us consider the first way. Yes, nobody spends money to become rich. Or, have you seen or heard anybody who comes forward to testify that he has spent so much money that he ended up rich in the process? Never! You don't spend money to become rich. In fact, the more you spend, the poorer you become.

But this does not mean that you cannot use your money to buy anything. Of course you must buy things with your money. But it is what you buy with your money that matters. Spending money means using your money to buy things that do not add value or bring returns to you. Spending money means buying liabilities. It means using your money to buy things that take money from you. For instance, when a young man who has no stable or regular income, and who is struggling financially, goes ahead to buy a small 5KVA generator, popularly called 'I pass my neighbour' in Nigeria, that generator will require him to buy fuel almost every other day, and to service it periodically, thereby taking money from him. Also in this age of information technology, many young people are buying and using GSM handsets that they ought not to have in the first place. And many of these young people who have no regular income whatsoever spend lots of money to subscribe to network service providers for air time and Internet services. Hence, these GSM handsets are liabilities that take money away from people, rather than bring money to them.

When you spend your money to buy liabilities in this way, it means you are throwing away your potential money trees that are supposed to give you more bread to eat and seeds to sow tomorrow. If you must spend your money, buy assets rather than liabilities. Assets bring money to you, while liabilities take money from you. Be wise!

Now, let us consider the second way. Nobody hoards money to become rich. Hoarding money means keeping the money to yourself alone; it means not allowing the money to go away from you; it means holding unto the money, and not allowing it to circulate.

When you hoard money, you are suffocating and killing your money seeds, and your money will not grow, increase or multiply that way. You are just like that unfaithful servant who received his talent and hid it in the ground. After many years, the talent did not increase beyond what he received from his master, because he hid it in the ground rather than allow it to circulate.

You see, money likes freedom and enjoys being allowed to circulate. It is only then that it can work for you and yield more money for you. Money is like the corn of wheat. "Except a corn of wheat fall into the ground and die, it abideth alone: but if it die, it bringeth forth much fruit." (John 12:24). So, you don't keep your money by holding unto it; rather, you keep your money by releasing it to go and work for you. This is the paradox of money. It is the mystery of money management.

The only reason why you should hold unto any portion of your money is to preserve and prepare it for the next planting season. And the next planting season, as far as money is concerned, is whenever a good investment opportunity comes; and it could be any time. So, always get your seeds ready for planting. And when you spot a good investment opportunity, don't hesitate or procrastinate, go ahead and release the seeds immediately into the soil for a future harvest. This is the way to grow and multiply your money in order to become rich.

Types of Soil for Growing Your Money

How much your money seed is worth depends on how long you allow it to grow and at what rate. Here are some soil upon which you could sow your money seeds and their expected rates of return:

1. Inside Pillow or Box or in the Ground – 0%
2. In a Savings Account – 2-5%
3. Fixed Deposit Account and Cooperative Society – 10-12%
4. Stocks and Mutual Funds – 10-20%
5. Real Estates, Oil and Gas, Precious Metals – 15-45%
6. The Kingdom of God – 30%, 60%, 100%

Importance of Saving

If you don't save, your future is not safe. Saving secures your future. What you save today multiplies tomorrow.

The goal of this book is to get you to change your attitude towards money and how to save and invest it. If I can get you to form the habit of saving and investing at least one dollar a day, I would have achieved my aim for writing this book, and I will be fulfilled as having impacted you and your future generations.

Saving should be a daily practice. If you spend money every day; then you should save money every day. Design or join a system or scheme that will enable you to save some money every day. Determine how much you can save daily – how many dollars or naira do you think you can save daily. Remember, the more the better, and the faster too.

Yes, saving is not an interesting thing to do; it is boring; it is dull; and it is hard. And that is why majority of people do not do it. It is much easier to spend money than to save it. But, hard as it may be; dull as it may be; and boring as it may be, it is more rewarding to save money than to spend it; because what you save today remains for you tomorrow. But what you spend today finishes today. Therefore, no matter what, just do it. Go ahead and save that money for your future greater rewards and fulfillment.

Guidelines for Saving and Investing

The veteran financial and investment advisor, Robert G. Allen, in his masterpiece, *Multiple Streams of Income,* has prescribed the following guidelines for saving and investing:

1. Defer gratification for now and live on less than you earn;
2. Invest the surplus;

3. Live by budget;
4. Avoid debt;
5. Build long-term security;
6. Be disciplined;
7. Overcome procrastination – every day you wait – every hour you delay – is like burning up your future money; and
8. Consistency is the key and watchword.

Anybody who is really interested in building significant wealth in his life time needs to adhere to these guidelines that are given by a man who has done what he is teaching.

7

Charting Your Way to Wealth through Borrowing & Lending

God does not encourage borrowing. This is clearly stated in His word:

> Owe no man any thing, but to love one another: for he that loveth another hath fulfilled the law. Romans 13:8

Here, we are commanded to owe no man anything. This implies that we are never to get indebted to anyone. The only thing we owe people around us is love; and we must endeavor to pay what we owe people if we are real children of God. Deuteronomy 28:12 clearly states:

> The Lord shall open unto thee his good treasure, the heaven to give the rain unto thy land in his season, and to bless all the work of thine hand: and

thou shalt lend unto many nations, and thou shalt not borrow.

Here, God forbids us to borrow on the basis of the abundant provision that He has made available to us. And this completely cancels out any reason or excuse that we may have for wanting to go into borrowing. He has promised to open unto us His good treasure; for the heaven to give rain unto our land in due season; and to bless the work of our hand. And God's faithfulness has ensured that this promise is being fulfilled upon us every passing day. That is why we always witness rainfall and sunshine in their due seasons; and that is why our seeds sown germinate, grow and bear fruits in their seasons; and that is why the works of our hands (our businesses and occupations) yield profits or income for us as and when due. So we really have no reason for borrowing.

Thou shall not borrow! This is the express command from God. We are not to debate it, but to obey it. Obeying this divine command is for our own good; and disobeying it is at our own peril. The reason for this, as stated in Proverbs 22:7, is:

> The rich ruleth over the poor, and
> the borrower is servant to the lender.

God, in his infinite love, does not want any of his children to become a servant to lenders; that is why he made adequate provisions for his children and forbids them from borrowing. Or, would you rather be a servant than be a master? The choice is yours.

It is necessary for us to correct an impression here – that, borrowing or buying things on credit is not a sin, but it is a weight that would make it difficult for you to pursue and fulfill your divine purpose. It is a weight that would make it difficult for you to serve God and do his will as you ought to. The reason is, you cannot serve two masters. At the time you are a servant to a lender, you are duty bound to do the will of your master. As a result, you will most probably find it difficult to do the perfect will of God, especially regarding handing your finances. This is why you and I must avoid borrowing and getting into debt like a plague.

There was a time I borrowed from the bank to clear the backlog of my school fees and sponsor my PhD defense. The loan was spread over three years (36 months). It is needless for me to say that those three years were some of the most perilous seasons of my life, as I was struggling to pay back the loan, to pay my house rent, to feed and take care of my family and to pay my tithe, give offering and fulfill other financial commitments in my church. My monthly income could not cover all these obligations, and I was practically living from debt to debt within those very long and tedious years. It was not interesting or palatable at all.

Please if you can help it, avoid borrowing or debts like a plague. Though it seems faster to borrow or to buy things on credit, it is better and safer to save.

> The thoughts of the diligent tend only to plenteousness; but of every one that is hasty only to want.

As we said earlier, borrowing or buying things on credit is not a sin, but is a weight. But not borrowing or not buying things on credit is wisdom.

> Better is a dry morsel, and quietness therewith, than an house full of sacrifices with strife.

Let us learn to be contented with what we have at any particular point in life. Life is in phases, and men are in sizes. And, as we are told in 1Timothy 6:6, "…godliness with contentment is great gain." Therefore,

> Let your conversation be without covetousness; and be content with such things as ye have: for he hath said, I will never leave thee, nor forsake thee. (Hebrews 13:5).

Specifically, "…be content with your wages" (Luke 3:14c). This is an admonition of our Lord Jesus Christ to us.

And if, peradventure, you do borrow or if you find yourself in debt, you should be committed to paying your debt; because you are commanded to owe no man. In Psalm 37:21, we are told that it is only a wicked man that would borrow and not pay back or return what he borrows. Debt repayment is always a very difficult thing to do. The reason is that at the time you are to repay the loan, there are always responsibilities that place a demand on the money with which you want to pay the debt. So the issue, most often, is not whether you have money on you with which to pay the debt or not; rather, it is always that there are pressing needs for the money at that particular time. But even at that, you must understand that repaying the loan is also an obligation that you must fulfill. Failure to do this, you stand to lose your integrity and dignity. And these are great virtues that you cannot afford to trade off. Therefore you must suspend all other obligations in order to pay off your debts. Or, better still, you can meet your creditor(s) and re-negotiate the terms and modes of repayment. But you must know that your creditor(s) is/are not duty bound to accept your new terms and modes of loan repayment.

THE BIBLICAL WAY TO BORROWING

In case you really need to borrow to take care of a very urgent important need, or for business purpose; or in case you need to buy goods on credit, there is a right or wrong way to borrow. The biblical way to borrow is to avoid surety.

What Is Surety?

Surety is assuming an obligation to pay indebtedness without a 'sure' way to pay it. It is a liability incurred from debt. Surety means that we presume upon the future – If everything goes as we expect, we will be able to pay the loan back. But if things go wrong, we may be left in debt.

Let us look at some case studies on surety:

Case Study 1:

When you borrow to marry a wife or bury a loved one, there is no certain way that is derivable from the usage of that loan that will enable you to repay the loan. This is surety.

What this means is that the new wife you are borrowing to marry or your dead relation that you are borrowing money to bury will not generate the money that would be needed to repay the loan. Hence, there is 100% surety. You must avoid this type of borrowing like a plague. It can ensnare you for life or for a very long time. Borrowing to feed, buy clothes, etc, also fall under this category of borrowing that you must avoid.

Case Study 2:

When you borrow to buy a car, the car is pledged as the collateral. But with time, the car depreciates in value and would not pay off the loan when you default; then you are liable to pay the deficiency. This is partial surety.

Some years ago, I bought a second or third hand Mercedes Benz 200 car at the rate of N120, 000.00. Because of its age, coupled with the fact that that class of Benz cars were being phased out, the car depreciated very fast. And when I desired to sell off the car three years later, it had become valueless. After much fruitless effort to get a buyer for it, I simply called the guys at the junkyard and they came to tow it away for dismantling. They paid me N12,000.00 for the car I bought N120,000.00 only three years ago! Now, assuming that I had borrowed the money by pledging the car as collateral, where would I have got the money to repay the loan? This is why surety is very risky.

Case Study 3

When you stand surety for somebody's debt, you have no certain way to repay the debt from the usage of that money. Hence you incur total liability in event of default.

Some years ago, there was this colleague of mine who took a bank loan and used another colleague as her guarantor. Unfortunately, things went wrong, as they often or sometimes do. The woman took suddenly ill and died shortly after taking the loan and using it for the purpose for which she took the loan. And, as expected, the bank came after the other woman who stood as a guarantor for the loan, just as the Bible prescribes in

Proverbs 27:13. And because she was not having a certain way to repay the loan, (since she was not the person who used the money), she started crying hysterically and running helter-skelter, looking for money to repay the debt she did not owe.

This scenario clearly illustrates Proverbs 11:15,

> He that is surety for a stranger shall smart for it: and he that hateth suretyship is sure.

Case Study 4

As a salary earner, when you borrow money against your salary, and the money is used for a purpose that cannot generate the money to repay the loan, and you use your salary to repay the loan, there is full surety. But when you borrow money for an investment or business deal that is able to generate the money to repay the loan without endangering your salary, there is no surety. But you must be very sure that the deal will not misfire.

Case Study 5

When you borrow to buy a land, the land is pledged as collateral. And with time the land appreciates in value that can pay off the entire loan and you still make profit. There is no surety here.

From the above case studies, it is clear that surety results when there is no certain way to pay the debt. And there is no surety if there is a certain way to pay the debt; and that certain way must be derived from the usage of the borrowed money.

Thus you can avoid surety by ensuring that the collateral you are pledging totally secures the loan. And, in case you are approached or tempted to stand as a guarantor or surety for someone who wants to borrow, here is what the scriptures say:

> Be not thou one of them that strike hands, or of them that are sureties for debts. If thou hast nothing to pay, why should he take away thy bed from under thee? Proverbs 22:26-27.

A word, they say, is enough for the wise. If you have been doing it before now in ignorance, as many of us have, please stop it. Don't stand surety for anybody's debts again. It is for your security and well-being.

BUSINESS BORROWING

From what we have discussed so far on the subject of borrowing and surety, it is clear that borrowing or buying things on credit is not a sin, but it is a weight; it is an indication of lack of faith in and patience with God; and it will rob you of the strength or ability to do the perfect will of God. Also, from the various case studies on suretyship presented above, it is clear that credit is not the problem, but the misuse of credit.

In the business world, it may be strongly argued that it is difficult to do business without borrowing. This may be true to a great extent, because the larger percentage of the businesses that are carried out in the world today are done through credit facilities. If not, the banks and many other financial institutions would neither exist nor be relevant. Yes, commerce is done mainly through credit. The reason is that it seems faster to borrow for business or buy goods and services on credit. But good wisdom says:

> The thoughts of the diligent tend only to plenteousness; but of every one that is hasty only to want. Proverbs 21:5.

Therefore, though business seems to move faster through borrowing or credit purchases or supplies, not borrowing is wisdom.

> Better is a dry morsel, and quietness therewith, than an house full of sacrifices with strife. Proverbs 17:1.

What this means is that you can run into muddy waters when you borrow to do business or when you buy things on credit, due to miscalculations or wrong projections.

Yes, borrowing on an asset that appreciates is good, but you must know that nothing appreciates forever. Also, you may not be able to predict when or how fast the item will appreciate. So be careful. Rather than allow your many years' labour collapse like a pack of cards through litigations that will come from your creditors who want to recover their money by all means, why not go slowly but surely. You can run your business debt-free. It only requires starting small and growing bigger slowly and steadily. It is better to have a solid foundation than quick growth. And you have a solid foundation when you start your business without borrowing. Building your business on borrowed money is like building your house on the sand. (Luke 6:48-49). The choice is yours.

LENDING

There is nothing glorious about being a borrower. I have been there, and I have confirmed that, "…the borrower is servant to the lender." (Proverbs 22:7). Rather than be a borrower, why not aspire to be a lender. God does not forbid His children from being lenders; rather, He encourages them along that line:

> The Lord shall open unto thee his good treasure, the heaven to give the rain unto thy land in his season, and to bless all the work of thine hand: and thou shalt lend unto many nations, and thou shalt not borrow. (Deuteronomy 28:12).

This clearly shows that God has made adequate provision for his children (Christians) to gain control of the world's economy and political power through the business of lending. Where the likes of World Bank, Paris Club,

Swiss Banks, etc, are occupying today in the global economy and political power, is where Christians are supposed to occupy by divine provision and ordination. But it seems we have sold our birthright, and we are now at their mercy. But, may God give us the grace and determination to free ourselves from slavery in the name of Jesus Christ. Amen.

So, lending is a good business, especially for Christians. Reasons for being a lender include:

1. To employ idle funds;
2. To make a profit, in the form of interests, dividends, etc.;
3. Because people have needs you can help meet;
4. Because people will always ask you for loan or credit facilities;
5. It is a weapon of control.

LENDING AND SOCIETY

No society operates without borrowing and lending. This is because borrowing and lending aid trade, commerce and development. Much of the development we see in the human society today is made possible through credit facilities. The reason for this is that no human being, corporate entity, government or nation has enough to take care of all pressing needs, however rich that person, institution, organisation, government or nation may be. This is why we see individuals, institutions, organisations, governments and nations going about, cap in hand, looking for credit facilities needed for execution of their developmental projects. And this is why any person, institution or organization that aspires to go into the lending business is sure to become very rich and powerful.

Because society encourages lending and borrowing, most laws governing the human society in general and nations in particular favour the borrowers over the lenders. This is in order to encourage borrowing and to protect borrowers from oppression. This, however, does not mean that lenders are not protected. Laws of society also provide that creditors can also employ lawful means to recover their money from their debtors, especially within the approved limited or unlimited liabilities.

BIBLICAL STANDPOINTS ON LENDING

As in the case of borrowing, the Bible establishes a base for lending. Proverbs 22:7 holds,

> The rich ruleth over the poor,
> and the borrower is servant to the
> lender.

Hence, God's word does not prohibit lending; rather, God promises us a surplus that we can loan out to enhance the prosperity of individuals and societal development.

But while it is desirous to be a lender, Christians must be sure to obey the law of giving first and foremost. Acts 20:35 clearly states, "It is more blessed to give than to receive." Therefore, it is an act of wickedness for a Christian to lend money to a fellow Christian, or even to an unbeliever who is in need of basic necessities of food, clothes, etc, when he is in position to help meet those needs. The Bible's position on this is, "…freely ye have received, freely give." (Matthew 10:8);

> Give to every man that asketh of thee; and of him that taketh away thy goods ask them not again…. And if ye lend to them of whom ye hope to receive, what thank have ye? for sinners also lend to sinners, to receive as much again (Luke 6:30,34).

This clearly establishes that the Christian money lender must be different from the non-Christian money lender. We have heard so many stories about some wicked money lenders who would go to the extent of casting spell on the people who borrow from them, to make it difficult or even impossible for them to gather money to repay their debts, thereby making their interest to accumulate so much that they become enslaved to these wicked money lenders. This is what the bible clearly forbids of Christian money lenders. Our ways should be very different from the ways of unbelievers, because we are children of God.

Thus, a Christian in the lending business can give loans with interest for business purposes; and he should charge moderate interests comparatively, and operate a system that would make it easy for his debtors to repay their debts. And, most importantly, such Christian money lenders should be very prudent not to extend credit to those who cannot reasonably repay it.

> A prudent man foreseeth the evil, and hideth himself; but the simple pass on, and are punished. (Proverbs 27:12).

SUMMARY

You can start a business without borrowing, but this requires starting small and growing big gradually. You can also start a business with borrowed fund, and this enables you to start big. But you must understand that starting a business without borrowing is like building your house on the rock – it gives your business a solid foundation. And starting your business on borrowed fund is like building your house on the sand – it may not withstand the storms of life.

You also have a choice between being a borrower, and aspiring to become a lender. If you choose to be a borrower, you have decided for poverty and to be a servant to the lender. But if you choose to become a lender, you have decided to become very rich and to gain control over the multitudes that will be borrowing from you. By becoming a lender, you have decided to reign on earth. The choice is yours!

8

Principles of Wealth Creation in Business

Statistics have revealed that only 5% of people in the work force retire independently wealthy, while a whopping 95% of people retire poor. The reasons for this scary statistics include:

1. They work for other people;
2. They work with their hands;
3. They sell their time; and
4. They spend all they earn, and some more.

In *The Quickest and Smartest Way to Make Money,* I took time to explain these four main reasons why people retire poor and dependent on others for their sustenance.

Whether you are an employee or a business person, it has been proved over the years that nobody works for others to become rich. To become rich, you must work for yourself. This means that even when you are an employee, you must develop a mentality in which you do not see yourself as working for anybody but yourself. It is this mentality that will enable you to transform yourself from an employee to a self-employed, and eventually to an employer of labour. Thus, from where you are now as an employee, make plans to sack your employer as soon as possible in order to employ yourself, and then to employ others; and you will see how easy and how fast you can become rich when you start working for yourself and when other people start working for you.

In *The Quickest and Smartest Way to Make Money,* I made reference to something that Brian Sher's father once told him, as recalled by him:

> I remember a statement my father once made: Never work with your hand – it will never make you rich.

And I explained that the reason for this is that there is a limit to how many things your hands can handle per time. Therefore, for you to become rich, you must find some ways to duplicate, replicate and multiply your hands. You can do that by getting people to work for you in one way or the other, even if they are not directly under your employment. The network marketing system has made this very possible these days. So why not put a system in place that would enable you to multiply your hands in some ways.

Another way you can take some work away from your hands is to use your head. This is one of the best advices ever given to man: Don't use your hands to work, use your head. It is your head that will move you ahead, not your hands. We are now living in an age where fewer and fewer people are using their head. The larger majority of people are so busy with their hands. They are no longer even working with their hands, which would have made it a bit pardonable. These days, people are having busy hands – hands that are busy at nothing important. Their hands are busy on key pads, pinging and chatting their destinies away. No wonder, the rate of poverty is increasing by the day.

Therefore if you must become highly productive and become very rich, you must disengage your hands and engage your head to work out your salvation from poverty into great prosperity with fear and trembling. Use your head to know what people want, and find a way of helping them to get what they want; and you are on your way to great wealth.

Another thing that people do to enslave themselves is that they sell their time for money. One thing I want you to know is that when you sell your time, you are making yourself less than other men around you who are not selling their time. The reason is that time is the only commodity of life that God gave to all men equally. Every man on earth has exactly twenty four hours per day within which to live his life. And when you sell out part of your twenty four hours, it means you are left with less than a full day each to live your life. For instance, when a man sells out eight hours per day to his employer, he does not have control over those eight hours; rather, he is left with sixteen hours. Some men work six to six or seven to seven, which means they have sold out twelve hours of their day to their employers. Some men, especially in the western world, even hold double jobs of eight hours each. What this means is that such people have sold out sixteen hours of their day to their employers, who pay them peanuts that can hardly pay their bills. The only time such people have left is the time they spend for eating and sleeping. Hence, such people are nothing but slaves. They waste their lives working for others with no more time to live their own lives. Most people who work in public service, private sector and private practice sell their time; and they live from hand to mouth, from debt to debt; and eventually retire poor and broke.

Another way that you can sell your time is when your productivity is tied to your personal efforts. There is a limit to how much you can achieve as an individual alone. Therefore, to tie your productivity to your personal efforts is to limit yourself greatly. It boils down to the need for you to find a way of removing your productivity from your personal efforts. Find a way to get your productivity going non-stop, whether you are present or absent, or whether you are sleeping or not. Let your business run on systems, rather than with your blood.

The forth reason why people retire poor is because they spend all they earn, and some more. One very important thing that every salary earner must urgently learn to do is to cut his coat according to the cloth he has.

My father in the Lord, Bishop David Oyedepo, enjoins everyone to live his size per time, because life is in phases and men are in sizes. Therefore when you live above your size, you have chosen to sacrifice your future on the altar of present gratification.

Everybody wants the good things of life, and nobody says that you cannot and should not get the good things of life. But in getting the good things of life, you should go for those things that match your size. Fortunately for us, the marketplace has been designed to sell goods and services of all sizes and prices. No matter how poor you are you will get things that match your size in the market; and no matter how rich you are, you will also get things that match your size in the market. So, instead of robbing yourself of your glorious future, why not look for the goods and services that are designed and tailor-made for your present status.

The reason why many of us go for goods and services that are above our levels is because we are always impatient and so much in a hurry to enjoy those things that are above our status; and in the process, we often end up not being able to climb or rise up to those higher statuses. There is a proverb in my local parlance, which says that the water that man would drink cannot flow beyond him. Therefore, patience is required for attaining the higher status in life, and consequently for enjoying the better things of life.

Whatever may be your level of earning, try not to spend above what you earn. Put in place a system that would enable you to spend below your earning; a system that would enable you to automatically save a percentage of your earning per pay check, thereby leaving you with less than 100% of your earning for your spending. The reason is that when you habitually spend all or more than what you earn, you will perpetually remain poor or live in debts. Let us be wise!

Principles of Wealth Creation

One of the principles of wealth creation that has been established over the ages is that nobody works for others to become rich. For you to become rich, you must work for yourself. This means that you need to go into business for yourself to become rich. But be warned! You will not become rich automatically when you go into business for yourself.

Statistics reveal that over 75% of people who go into business for themselves always fail out of it. The reason for this is that most people rush into business without first getting it right. So you need to get it right first before going into any business. In other words, you need to start a business with the right attributes, if you hope to succeed in business. It is not every business that has the ability to make you rich; in fact most business has the tendency to make you poorer, rather than make you richer. Therefore you must be very careful if you are planning to go into business for yourself.

In *The Quickest and Smartest Way to Make Money,* I examined some of the right business attributes that have been prescribed by Brian Sher. Because of their great importance, let us briefly re-examine them here.

1. Never Build a Business; Build a Valuable Asset to Sell – The business you start should grow to become valuable to someone else in order to make you rich. Your focus should not be to build a business that would remain yours and your offspring's' forever. That is the traditional way of building a business. Most businesses that are built in this traditional way often become obsolete and end up as liabilities or family museums after two or three generations. In these modern days, it has become more beneficial to start and build a business that would become valuable to someone else, which you can sell in order to make you rich.

What this means is for you to organize the business in a way to make it appreciate and become a valuable asset you can sell for a great price and become rich.

This means that you must minimize the sentimental attachment to your business that would make it difficult or impossible for you to sell out the business when the time is ripe for a sellout. Yes, while you are at it, you must put everything into your business to build it to become a very valuable asset. But when this is done, and it is time to sell out, don't delay a minute longer because of personal attachment to your business. See the business as a valuable asset that is being offered for sale. At that point, you either sell the business and walk away with your billions or trillions or you hold unto it and it depreciates, never to rise to that point again; and, of course, you lose your money and end up with a liability for ever. Please know that business is no longer being built for keeps; it is now being built for sale.

2. Package and Leverage Your Time for Money – Don't go into a business that requires you to sell your time or make money from your personal effort. Leveraging your time in business includes making the product once and selling it again and again. Leveraging your time allows you to earn 10, 100 or even 1000 times. Such products as books,

music albums, home videos, CDs, DVDs, etc, that you make once and sell over and over again enable you to leverage your time and earn very many times from the same products.

3. Build a Network of People Who will Work for You – Operate your business through systems. This is because your efforts alone will never amount to much. Can you imagine yourself alone on a desert with a vast expanse of sand dunes? How much of the sand can you pack in your two hands? This is what many of us do in life. We are in a world that is filled with so much abundance. But what many of us do is that we individually try to use our hands alone to gather from the great abundance. Unfortunately for us, what our small hands can gather is so limited in the face of the great abundance that is available to us. Therefore anybody who wants to gather much from the available abundance in life must multiply his hands by borrowing other people's hands to gather as much as possible. You do this when you operate your business through systems.

Systemizing your business will enable you to make money from the efforts of everyone in your business. Systemizing your business will enable you to 'free' your time, such that whether you are present or absent, the system will keep on making money for you. Systemizing your business will enable you to sleep peacefully or even take a vacation or retire early from active service and yet somebody, somewhere, unknown to you is working for you, and your money is just rolling in. The opportunities in network marketing and the internet technology have made this very possible today. Take advantage of them.

4. Have interest in what you do. Having interest in what you do serves as a propelling force that will enable you to succeed in life. Along this line, Kenny Rogers advises, "Love what you do, have somebody to love and have a future to look forward to." This means that in addition to having interest in what you do, you need to have somebody you love, a beneficiary for whom you are ready to go the extra mile to make it in life. Also, you need to envision a great and glorious future for which you are ready to sacrifice any present comfort or pleasure. In a nutshell, establish your ultimate beneficiary or the end result of your wealth.

5. Conserve what you have. On this, James et al advise:

> When the money starts coming in, don't just spend more – live by your budget, eliminate debt, accumulate a cash reserve, invest

wisely for the future (retirement and other future plans), and, of course, help others.

The secret keys for conserving what you have are prudence and frugality. Prudence is being cautious and wise in conduct; being discreet; showing or having forethought. Prudence is application of wisdom to practice. To a large extent, therefore, prudence means thinking before acting. In other words, a prudent man does not just do things, but he takes his time to think through before going into action. That is, he looks before he leaps. Much of the problems we have landed ourselves at one time or the other would have been avoided if we had been a little more prudent.

Frugality is the other secret key for conserving our resources. Frugality means economy or thrift. Being frugal means being economical in the use of means; it also means sparing. Man is extravagant in nature. When anything enters his hands, he immediately thinks of ways to consume, spend or waste it. This is why nothing ever lasts or is ever enough in the hand of a natural mind. And this is also why man's expenses naturally rise above his income, according to Parkinson's Law of Income and Expenses. Therefore any man who would conserve his resources and become rich and wealthy must develop the ability to break Parkinson's Law of Income and Expenses; which holds that a person's expenses tend to rise to equate his income. And the best and most workable advice that has been given to us by authorities is the 80/20 Pareto Principle, which, among other prescriptions, recommends that you save and invest at least 20% of every income persistently to generate 80% of your wealth. A practical application of this principle to your finances will surely make much difference in your march towards prosperity. Therefore, engage in safe and wise investment continuously.

6. Have the right attitude towards money. The lure of money and material things has a very strong hold on man. All the unmitigated atrocities that we witness in the human societies are all testimonies to the alluring effect of money on man. Thus, in order not to be destroyed by the love of money, which is the root of all evils, we must, by all means, avoid the lure of money and material riches. We must apply self-control and some financial common sense in order to gain control over money and riches. We must know that there are things that are more valuable than money. Failure to do this would result in the loss of what money cannot buy. It is better to lose our money than for us to lose what money cannot buy. Let us be very careful.

The Kind of Business that Makes Money

The best and fastest way to make money is to go into business for yourself. But it is insightful for us to understand that it is not every business that has the ability to make money for you. Some businesses are as good as pure waste of time. Therefore when going into business, you must take time to consider the kind of business you go into. Unless you go into the right business, you stand a chance of losing all your money. In fact, it is better not to go into business so as to keep your money, rather than go into business and lose your money in the process.

FACTORS TO CONSIDER WHEN GOING INTO BUSINESS

In setting up a business that will make you money, there are factors to consider, which include:

1. Identify an opportunity that is linked to your 'occupational sweet spot'. This means you are to develop a business out of your gifts, dreams, interests, skills, talents, passions, hobbies, etc. Ability to do this will make your work fun.

2. Choose a business that is in line with your interest or passion. It is in respect of this that Confucius admonishes: "Choose the work you love and you will never have to work a moment in your life."

3. Identify an opportunity that will allow you to create the life you want – one that will provide the level of income that can support the lifestyle you want to have – that will pay your bills.

4. Select an opportunity with high upside and low downside. This means that you should select a business opportunity that will require little capital to start, but that guarantees high profitability. Very many businesses are highly capital intensive, but are more or less worthless. Run away from these. On the other hand, there are businesses that require very little capital, but which are very lucrative. Look out for these kind of businesses and invest in them. Examples of businesses with low downside and high upside include real estate, consultancy, writing, counseling (financial, marriage, career, etc), insurance, agency, stockbroking, personal trainers, care provision, service provision, etc.

Steps to Starting a New Business

The followings are some steps prescribed by Brian Sher, that you will need to take in setting up a new business:

1. Identify a business that has a limited downside and a significant upside – as has just been explained in (4) of the previous section above. This reduces business risk.

2. Conduct a thorough feasibility study. Research the viability of that kind of business in your locality. It amounts to waste of resources to start a business with so much capital only to find out afterwards that the business is not viable in that locality. You can avoid this by first carrying out a thorough feasibility study before committing your scarce resources into the business. Remember, all that glitters is not gold. Consult an expert who will help conduct a good feasibility study for your proposed business.

3. Develop a business plan and a time table. It is foolishness to start a business without a practicable business plan and a time table or work schedule. These should serve as the blueprints for the running of your business. This will enable you to operate your business according to a pre-planned schedule. You can also consult a professional business planner to help you draw a good business plan.

4. Jump in! Do it! Leap while looking. Once you have identified a potential business with a limited downside and a significant upside; you have done a good feasibility study; and you have drawn a workable business plan/time table; the next thing to do is to stop vacillating. Jump in and start work immediately. Throw open the doors of your

business and let the world know what you have to offer.

Of course, at the beginning, everything will not be set, but you must get started all the same. You cannot afford to wait till everything is set, because that will never happen. Therefore once you have met the minimum requirements for starting your business, you must go ahead and leap while looking to set the other things in order. And don't be afraid to start small, because that is how big corporations and multinationals are made.

5. Talk, talk and talk about what you are doing. Motivational authorities have established: "A closed mouth is a closed destiny." The most powerful marketing tool has been identified as the mouth. Until you talk to people about what you are doing, nobody knows what you have to offer. Doing business without talking to people about your business is like a man who is blinking in the dark; he knows what he is doing, but nobody else does. Therefore, rise up, go out and start talking to people about your business. And remember, if you can't blow your own trumpet, don't expect other people to blow it for you. In business, you are your own prompter and trumpeter. Go ahead and blow!

6. Execute your business with excellence. This is what will make your business to stand out above

your competitors. Don't run your business shabbily, run it with distinction, and your business will be distinguished.

Qualities of Successful Businesses

For your business to succeed tremendously, you must learn to do the followings:

1. Deliver high value-added services.

   Your business cannot stand out unless it delivers outstanding services. If you do business the same way every other person around you does his business, people will not see any reason to move from your competitors to do business with you. The only reason why people will want to do business with you is because of the high and exceptional value-added services that your business offers.

2. Incorporate in-depth-focused knowledge.

   Do not carry out your business with ignorance. This is where the need for continuous reading and research comes in. Commit to continuous learning and development in your business area. As much as possible, enroll and go for regular training programmes to update your knowledge. Also, train your staff or send them out for regular training, if you don't want to stand the risk of your business practices becoming obsolete. Even if you are the only staff in your business, set up a Research and Development (R&D) Department that is responsible for keeping your business abreast of facts. It will help to keep your business up-to-date and relevant in the scheme of things, and this will continue to affect your bottom line positively.

3. Serve a large and growing market.

   Show me your target market, and I will show you where your business is headed. Your market is your business. If you serve a small and limited market, then you will end up with a small and limited business; but when you serve a large, unlimited and growing market, then you are sure to end up with a big, unlimited and growing business. I don't see why anybody in Nigeria should target a small market. The Nigerian populace is one of the largest markets for any business in the world. This is why, despite the security and some other unhealthy situations in Nigeria, foreign investors are still rushing in and signing investment deals with the Nigerian Government. Nigerian citizens should also catch in on the large and growing Nigerian market and come out with some unique products and services, rather than continue to hide behind the excuses of unemployment and joblessness. Also, every businessman worth his salt should take advantage of the large and growing Nigerian market to grow his business to an enviable height in Nigeria. This is because we have what it takes to build great businesses in Nigeria – we have the human, material, financial and natural resources in great abundance! What else are we waiting for? Let us go to work and raise great corporations and multinationals that will make Nigeria to take its pride of place among the committee of nations!

4. Make your product once and sell it over and over again.

Great businesses value their time. They don't waste their time by selling it; rather, they leverage their time by making their products once and selling them over and over and over again. Check your product. If you have to spend time to produce it every time it is required, then it is not a good product. If, for instance, you are a potter, and you have to sit down personally to make a pot for each customer who places an order, then you will hardly get rich in that business, because you don't have a great product. But if, on the other hand, you are a singer, and you go into the studio to produce your album once, which you sell over and over to every music lover who wants it, then you have a great product that can make you rich. What makes a great product is that it does not require you to sit down to make the product each time it is demanded; rather, it is produced once, and you keep selling it over and over again. Now check out your product; do you have a poor product or a great product? In that case, you don't need any soothsayer to tell you whether your business will succeed or not.

5. Make your business valuable and saleable.

Times have changed. People are no longer building family businesses that they will pass on to their next generations. People are now building valuable businesses that they can sell to become rich. Sorry, we are no longer in the days of companies and corporations; we are now in the days of valuable products and services. Therefore, rather than focus on building a liability, please focus on building an asset that you can easily convert to cash. Make your business valuable and saleable, and you are on your way to wealth.

6. Organize your business in such a way that your personal presence is not needed.

If you have organized your business in such a way that you cannot take a nap or a vacation, then you are hanging on a noose that will likely kill you. You don't need to commit suicide by hanging your business on yourself. You can take the noose off your neck and hang it on a system that will enable your business to run itself. Find a way to systemize your business, and you will be as free as air, and as rich as Solomon in the Bible. Ask yourself this question: Can your business operate successfully without your personal involvement? If your answer is, NO, then you must stop operations immediately, and then organize your business into a system that will run itself henceforth. This is the great and latest way to run a business profitably these days.

7. Put in place a very resourceful management team that is capable of smart financial thinking – one that takes advantage of good investment opportunities that enhance cash flow. You may have a great product and a great system; but if you have a dull or bad management team, your business will stand the risk of being strangulated and of dying pre-maturely. Therefore take your time to select a great management team that is made up of smart thinkers and swift actors. In very many cases, the management is the business, good or bad.

8. Build your business before you build your ideal lifestyle.

In this part of the world (the black race) we seem to have adopted the habit of setting the cart before the horse; and that is why we've not been able to get anywhere. The reason is obvious: when the cart is put before the horse, the horse can only stumble against the cart and fall. No wonder, many African nations and people are stumbling and falling. The reason why the larger majority of businesses in this region of the world are falling is because our businessmen are putting the cart before the horse. To succeed in business, you must learn to build your business first before building your lifestyle.

When you use the money (capital) that you are supposed to use for building your business to build a lifestyle for yourself, you succeed in killing your business. Let's be patient; if your business succeeds, you will surely have that lifestyle that you desire for yourself. But if your business fails, you will not be able to sustain the lifestyle that you have established for yourself. And the consequence is that, you will either lose both the business and the lifestyle, or you will begin to steal and engage in fraudulent practices in order to sustain the lifestyle. This is the reason for the high level of corruption in our nations today. But we can stop this trend by focusing on our businesses first before building our ideal lifestyles.

HOW TO LAUNCH YOUR NEW PRODUCT AND SERVICES

One great way to make it in life is to have something to offer. If you have nothing to offer, the world will not have any reason to patronize you. But when you have something to offer, the world will have no option than to look out for you and bring their substance to you. Look for something to offer the world.

Most often, what you have to offer could be in the form of a product or service. But having a product or service is not an absolute guarantee that you will make it, no matter how great the product or service may be. There are individuals and companies that have very great products and services, yet they are struggling or going into bankruptcy. The reason is obvious. Until you launch your product or service and bring it to the forefront of people (especially potential buyers), your great product or service may as well remain with you alone. I have some experience of this. I have written and self-published some great books that have remained packed and piled up in cartons both in my house and in my office, year in year out, with nobody caring to know what is in those cartons. And until I do something about launching those books and bringing them to the awareness of potential buyers, those books will continue to remain in those cartons and boxes until they become outdated or destroyed by worms and termites. Having a great product or service is not enough; you must launch your product and make it available to buyers and end users. This is where marketing comes in.

Marketing is the tool that drives your business. When it is used correctly, it is the biggest profit-making and money-making tool in business. Skillful marketing is the key that builds your business into success and profitability.

What Is Marketing?

Marketing is, knowing what your customers want and helping them to get it. Marketing is not about your product or service. It is focusing on your customers' needs rather than on your product or service. People don't really care about what you have; they care more about what they want. They want to solve their problems; and they are looking for what will help them to solve their problems. So if it is your product or service that will help them to solve their problem, they go for it. Or if it is your competitor's product or service that will help them solve their problem better, they go for it and leave you to your fate. Customers are not interested in you and your business, neither are they interested in what is important to you and your business. They only want something that answers their needs. And if you have what will answer their needs, then they patronize you without thinking about you. So it boils down to the age-long saying that, people don't care about what you have until they have what they want.

Another version of the above saying is, people don't care about what you know until they know how much you care. This reflects another aspect of marketing, which is caring about what your customers want. A very important aspect of marketing is, helping your customers to buy.

Getting your customers to buy is selling, while helping your customers to buy is marketing. The difference is in the manner of approach. You can get people to buy from you by adopting all manners of gimmicks, including sweet-tonguing, trickery, fear appeal, threat, wooing, cajoling, lying, deception, etc. In this case, you are focusing on your product rather than on the needs of your customers. And when you get people to buy from you in any of these ways, the people will most likely end up dissatisfied with you and your product; in which case, they will most likely not buy from you again or recommend you and your business to others. On the other hand, you may focus on what your customers want and help them to get it, even to the point of helping them get it from a fellow seller of the product or service when you do not have what they want at that particular time. When you help them to buy in this way, you end up with a friend and a loyal customer who will keep buying from you and recommend you and your business to others.

Marketing, therefore, means making yourself and your product or service available to your customers or potential customers, and helping them to meet their needs. It begins with creating awareness about your products; because people don't know about your good product or service until you market it to the right market at the right time to meet the right needs of the right customers. The statement we have just made above talks about four aspects of right marketing, which are:

1. Marketing to the right market;
2. Marketing at the right time;
3. Marketing to meet the right needs; and
4. Marketing to the right customers.

Let us briefly examine these four aspects of right marketing one by one.

1.   Marketing to the Right Market

Not every market is a right market for your products and services. The question to ask here is, What makes a market right or wrong? Here are some of the criteria that help to ascertain the rightness or wrongness of a market:

1. The size of the market: Is the market a small or big market?
2. The dynamics of the market: Is the market a growing market or a stable market?
3. The nature of the market: Is the market a volatile, trendy or traditional market? Do people in the market desire or respond readily to change or do they prefer the status quo?

Most often, the bigger the market, the better it is for your business. Also, the faster the growth of the market the faster the growth of your business as well. So a good business man must take time to determine the size and rate of growth of the market he is reaching out to. The business man must also determine the nature of the market; that is, he must know whether the market is a volatile, trendy or traditional one. This would enable him to determine whether the nature of his products or services fit into the market; and where the reverse is the case, the knowledge of the nature of the market would enable the businessman to tailor or customize his products and services to fit into the market

2. Marketing at the Right Time

In marketing, right timing is a key factor. This is more so when we consider that some markets are seasonal markets. A manufacturer or seller of products like umbrellas, rain coats, rain boots, etc, for instance, should know that his products are seasonal products that are useful to people only in the rainy season. So he will tailor his production and marketing to the rainy season. Also, some products and services sell better in the early hours of the day. A newspaper publisher, for instance, should know that people desire and hunt for latest news in the early hours of the day, and should therefore tailor his marketing efforts to the early hours of the day for greater patronage. A good businessman should also know that people have greater purchasing power at the beginning of the month than at the middle or towards the end of the month; and he should therefore channel his marketing efforts towards getting more people to buy his products and services at this time when people have more money to spend. Thus, the importance of right timing in marketing cannot be over-emphasized.

3.   Marketing to Meet the Right Needs

Marketing, as we said earlier, is finding ways to meet the needs of your customers, and making them to know that you have the solution to their problems. So, the target of right marketing is to meet the right needs. In Economics, we were told that human wants are uncountable and insatiable. Hence, any marketing effort that is aimed at attempting to satisfy human wants amounts to waste of time, efforts and resources. Rather, good marketing should target needs; and not just all needs, but the right needs. A good marketer should know that people's financial resources and purchasing power are limited. And most often, people can only take care of the most important and the most pressing needs in their lives. Therefore, the marketing efforts that are targeted at meeting the basic needs of man are likely to be right marketing. And in meeting these needs, the marketer is not to assume, but take time to study his customers and get to know what is most important and most pressing to them, as well as get to know the customers' purchasing power in order to help meet these particular needs of the customers. This is how to meet the right needs of customers.

4.   Marketing to the Right Customers

Any businessman who targets everybody in the world as his target market at any one particular time is sure to fail. The reason is that there is no business person or organization that has all the resources or marketing tools to reach out to the whole world at any one particular time. So even if a business organization has the vision of reaching to the whole world as a long term goal, it must do it one chunk at a time. This is where the need to reach out to the right customers comes in.

What makes the right customers are the people or people-groups that will find your products or services most useful to them; as well as the people who have the highest purchasing power and effective demand for your products or services. Hence, what is expected of a business person, organization or marketer is to study the general market in relation to taste or desire for his products or services. In doing this, attention should be paid to the various ways that the products or services would help meet the specific need of people. When this is properly and effectively done, the business person, organization or marketer would be able to identify and isolate the right customers for his products or services; after which all machinery would be put in motion towards reaching out to these identified and isolated customers. Spending so much efforts, time and money to reach out to wrong customers who will not buy your products or services amounts to waste.

ELEMENTS OF GOOD MARKETING

Some of the elements of good marketing that have been identified by authorities in the field include:

1. Understanding your customers;
2. Empathizing with your customers;
3. Relating to your customers;
4. Loving your customers;
5. Helping your customers in every way;
6. Contributing to your customers' lives; and
7. Adding value to your customers in every transaction.

Every good business person should know that he is not in business to sell products and services, but to solve people's problems. According to Brian Sher,

> To become rich, you must become a master of recognizing people's needs and desires, and of finding ways to satisfy them. If you can consistently do that quicker, cheaper, better, more conveniently, and with more trustworthiness and honesty than anyone else, you can't help but make a lot of money.

Get to know your customers – become intimate with them. This will enable you to design accurate strategies, effective marketing and productive advertising campaigns.

People will always be willing to pay you if you satisfy their needs and desires. Don't focus on money, if you must make money in business. Focus on giving value to your customers; that is, be value-driven, not money-driven. Money is a by-product of delivering value to people. People want value and are ready to pay for it. So if you want to be rich, don't try to make money; just add value to people's lives.

HOW TO BECOME A MARKETING GENIUS

The question to ask here is, what can make one a marketing genius? And the answer to this question is, ask your customers what they want and then take it one step further. But, before you rush ahead to ask your customers what they want, first sit down and ask yourself what you really want.

Yes, you want to be a genius in marketing, so that your products and services could be in high demand, and begin to make waves in the marketplace. What does it mean to be a genius at anything? According to *Longman Dictionary of Contemporary English,* a genius is "Someone who has an unusually high level of intelligence, mental skill or artistic ability." The same dictionary says, to be a genius at something or to have genius for (doing) something is, "to be especially good at doing something." Hence, genius is, as defined in the same dictionary, "a very high level of intelligence, mental skill, or artistic ability, which only few people have." If you want to be a genius in marketing, then you need to have a very high level of intelligence, mental skill and artistic ability with which to attract people to your business, and get them to buy from you or patronize you again and again. And the starting point, as we said earlier, is to ask your customers what they want and then take it one step further. In other words, the focus of a marketing genius is the customer and what he wants.

To know what your customers want, you need to get closer to them; you need to go out and sit face to face with them, and listen to their complaints and opinions. By your customers here, we do not mean only those who buy from you, but also those who do not buy from you, but from your competitors. I've seen some business people treat some people roughly and shabbily, simply because the people are not buying from them. In most cases, these people that are treated roughly have been identified as customers to their competitors. This is where business people often miss it. That a person is not buying from you now, or is currently buying from your competitor, does not mean he is not your customer. The customer may not be buying from you now for reasons best known to him. But you must be intelligent enough to know that, one day, your competitor will run out of stock of the product or service or he may not be around or the customers may no longer be satisfied with his product or service, and then the customer will be forced by such circumstances to come and buy from you. But if, all along, you have treated him shabbily or disrespectfully because he has not been buying from you, then rather than turn around to buy from you, the person will prefer to walk a distance down or up the road to buy from another seller of the same product or service, and you will lose a customer.

So, marketing intelligence requires you to know that those people who are not buying from you today are still your potential customers, and you need to treat them well. Therefore you must devise a way to reach out to the people who come in contact with your products or services but do not buy from you. Even when people did not buy from you, try to show them some courtesy; put in some kind word and even offer to be of assistance to them in some ways, if and when the need arises. Also, find out, in some ways, why they did not buy from you, and address the issue creatively and with maturity.

Listen to your customers and potential customers' complaints, opinions and suggestions. Provide a lot of care, and show great understanding. Let your customers see your willingness to change for the better or improve towards meeting their needs in their own terms. And where it is difficult to meet their condition or terms (customers could be very unreasonable and inconsiderate sometimes), take time to explain to them or educate them, and get them to see reasons with you or to understand your predicaments. When you do these, your customers or potential customers will see yours as a company that cares, and they will do everything possible to dump your less caring competitors and come to buy from you or do business with you; and they will even help to advertise your business by telling their families, friends and neighbours about your great products, services and customer service.

9

Essentials of Customer Service

Every dukedom has her duke; every empire has her emperor; every kingdom has her king. In all of these sovereign entities, there are various ways in which the subjects give reverence to their sovereign lords or monarchs. Some bow the head before their kings; others go on their knees before their sovereign lords; while some other subjects believe that their monarchs deserve no other way of reverence than prostrating flat before them. In all of these, it is not really the modes of giving reverence to the sovereign lords that matter; rather, what matters is that the subjects recognize the sovereign position of their lords, and have developed some ways of expressing that recognition. In all, the subjects have the mind to give reverence to and worship their sovereign lords for the lordship positions they occupy.

If actually every kingdom has her king, then the business world cannot be an exception. Every business owner needs to know that the business world is also a kingdom which has her own king. And the king of the business world is no other person than the customer. But though many business owners often say that the customer is the king, their attitude towards the customer often reveals that they are merely paying lip service. If, indeed, business owners recognize the customer as the king of their business, then their attitude towards the customer must not be short of reverence or worship to the king; because, every king deserves his worship.

The day a business owner recognizes that the customer is the king of his business, and begins to express this recognition by reverencing and worshipping the customer, that is the day his business, and even his own life, reaches a watershed. But the business owner who refuses to acknowledge the kingship position of his customers, and hence refuses to give them their well-deserved reverence, is doing nothing less than digging a grave for his business, and even for his own life.

I happen to have had a stint in commercial photography in my undergraduate and postgraduate days. In photography, we receive a lot of insults from unsatisfied customers. Even people who are far below us in age, in educational attainment and in social status tend to disrespect and even insult us. Well, that is the nature of the job (job hazard, you may say), and it is rather unfortunate. And the truth is that, at times, we find it very difficult to belly some of the customers' outrageous insults. At such times, we tend to reverberate, throw some of the insults back at those insolent customers and tell them to go to blazes with their money. At such times, we often feel good with ourselves, thinking that such very naughty customers deserve to be put in their proper positions. But the truth, nevertheless, remains that the customer, however outrageously rude he is, is the king. Take it or leave it! This, for many business owners, is a very bitter pill to swallow.

The reason why every business owner should see the customer as the king of his business is because it is the presence of the customer that determines the existence of the business. And, Kristin Anderson and Ron Zenke aver, "if you don't have customers, you don't have a job" or a business. Therefore, what every worthwhile business owner ought to do in order to prosper in his business is to ensure adequate and satisfactory customer service.

What is Customer Service?

To Richard F. Gerson, "customer service involves all the activities your business and employees conduct or perform to satisfy customers." ("Developing Superior Customer Service Programme" 18). Gerson is understood to hold that, you as a business owner must endeavor to sell your customers quality products to win them over, after which you must provide superior customer service to keep them. Thus customer service is more than just producing high quality products for your customers. Customer service also means going out of your way for the customer and doing everything possible to satisfy the customer and making decisions that benefit the customer even at the expense of your company.

Gerson strongly believes that providing customer service can be the critical difference in your company's success, especially in today's volatile economy. This opinion cannot, in any way, be faulted by any well-meaning business owner. In fact, today's entrepreneurs are to be reminded that they are not there to sell their products but to serve the customers. Thus customer service should first be considered before product sale. In the first place, customers will not buy the product if they are not satisfied. Therefore entrepreneurs should endeavor to ensure or even surpass customer satisfaction. In other words, they should be customer-oriented.

Steps to a Successful Customer Service System

Gerson has supplied us with seven steps to a successful customer service system, which are:

Step 1: Total Management Commitment

Top management must be committed to the concept of customer service. Then, management must communicate that vision as the company's service mission statement to all employees.

Step 2: Get to Know Your Customers

Get to know your customers, and also understand them. Know what they like, what they dislike, what they want changed, how they want it changed, what need they have, what their expectations are, what motivates them to buy, what satisfy them and what you must continue to do to maintain their loyalty. Simply ask them for this information.

Step 3: Develop Standards of Quality Performance

Each business practices standards of service that could be improved upon. When standards are set for ordinary business practices, you can be assured of superior performance by your employees.

Step 4: Hire, Train and Compensate Good Staff

If you want your business to be good to people, hire good people. Then train them to provide the ultimate in customer service and retention. Compensate them well because they are the primary contact your customers have with your company. These people are your company in the eyes and minds of the customers. Give your staff the authority to make decisions on the spot to satisfy customers.

Step 5: Reward Service Accomplishments

Always recognize, reward and reinforce superior performances. Provide financial and psychological rewards and incentives for your people. You must also reward your customers for good customer behaviour.

Step 6: Stay Close to your Customers

Always stay in touch with your customers. Develop a customer council to advise you on their needs, and listen to them. Customer interactions must be on win-win basis.

Step 7: Work towards Continuous Improvement

You must continuously work to improve your customer service and retention programmes. You must constantly work to provide the best service at all times. Your only goal for being in business should be to satisfy your customers.

("Developing Superior Customer Service Programme" 19-20).

These seven steps advanced by Richard F. Gerson seem to cover all there is to be said in customer service. And Gerson seemingly ratifies Customer Service with this:

Poor customer service is expensive. Good customer service is invaluable, and you can achieve it in your company. First, you must realize that service is both a marketing and management tool for your business...

Next, develop a customer service system for your company that is easy for your customer use...

design and implement customer retention programmes that will maintain customer loyalty (19).

THE BEST SELLING PRINCIPLE

As someone once said, business is a lot like tennis – those who don't serve well end up losing. Therefore a business person must make helping customers the top priority on the list of his business activities. Michael LeBeouf believes that "He who goes out to help his fellow man to a happier and easier way of life is exercising the highest type of salesmanship" (How to Win Customers and Keep them for Life" 22).

Thus the ultimate question for any business owner and his employees, as suggested by LeBeouf, is "How can I be of greater help to our customers?" In other words, entrepreneurs and employees must focus on what customers want and need, and find ways of helping them to buy what is best for them in order to make them feel good about it.

The whole idea of the best selling principle is based on the age-long issue of sowing and reaping; wherein, you reap what you sow. Just as it is in the general principle of life, in business you also get what you give. LeBeouf expresses this in his belief that "Sooner or later, the money and satisfaction you receive will be proportional to the service you render to others" (22). There is therefore no way we can over-emphasize the need for you to give the best of your service in order to reap the best reward in terms of higher profits and greater satisfaction.

TOWARDS CUSTOMER SATISFACTION

Kristin Anderson and Ron Zanke express an obvious fact:

Customers are demanding. And they have every right to be. Today's customers have more options than ever before. If your organization doesn't offer what they want or need, if you do not interact with them in a manner that meets or exceeds their expectations, they will just walk down the street or let their fingers walk through the Yellow Pages – and do business with one of your competitors ("You Are the Company" 24).

The factuality of this is enough to make every business owner to sit up and find ways of satisfying the demands of his customers.

And it should be of interest to business people that customers' perception of service is often unique, idiosyncratic, emotional, irrational, end-of-the-way and totally human. Therefore entrepreneurs and their employees must do all that is within their power and resources to study and understand the way customers perceive and react to their service. Customers are never to be taken for granted. It is not what you offer or what you think you are offering that matters; rather, what matters most is the customers' perception of your service.

You must therefore work as hard as possible in order to deliver more than yours customers' expectation, and in order to impress their perception.

In order to understand customers' perception of their service, many of "today's businesses collect or sort customer letters and comments cart looking for the complaints and the compliments that provide clues about what people want today, and how their needs may change" (Anderson and Zanke, 24). Anderson and Zanke are of the view that employees are not only to frequently draw on the knowledge their companies have acquired about customers, but they are also to make use of the information that they acquire from their day-to-day contact with the customers. These information range from what the customers want, which action meets their expectations, which exceeds them and which disappoints them. This information range, Anderson and Zanke believe, is the foundation on which the employees can build their own unique way of relating with the customers and providing knock-your-socks-off service (24). The more customers that are satisfied with your product or service will determine whether your business will survive or not.

CUSTOMER SERVICE/SELF-IMAGE

Central to the issue of customer service is that of self-image. Michael LeBeouf strongly believes that boosting the customer's self-image is the most effective way of making a positive and lasting impression on him. The reason for this is probably not unconnected with the potent force that is inherent in the preservation of self-image.

"For better or worse we are attracted to people and situation that confirm what we believe or want to believe about ourselves" (LeBeouf, 23). This is a basic truth of human nature. Thus every customer that comes your way wants or needs to have his self-image confirmed or boosted. It is therefore needless to stress that every entrepreneur or employee needs to tactfully identify his customers' self-image and concentrate on building such self-image. LeBeouf opines, "Every time you boost a customer's self-image you make a significant deposit to the emotional bank account and increase the odds of winning and keeping him" (23).

On how to significantly boost customers' self-image, Michael LeBeouf suggests five steps:

1. Develop a genuine interest in and admiration for your customers. IBM Founder, Thomas Watson, holds this view: "If you don't genuinely like your customers, the chances are they won't buy". In good customer relation, a good rule of the thumb, as suggested by LeBeouf, is to let the customer do 80 per cent of the talking. He believes that people are much more likely to buy when they are talking than when you are talking.

2. Recognise and praise people for what they want to be recognized and praised for. Tact is the art of seeing people as they wish to be seen. Give sincere and specific compliments. If possible, find a way to compliment the customer for something that results from having used your products and services in the past. Compliment him on being intelligent enough to take advantage of the benefits your business offers.

3. Put them at ease and establish rapport. We all prefer the company of people who make us feel accepted and relaxed.

4. Use humour where it's relevant and appropriate. Laughter is a tremendous influential tool. And influence is the name of the game when it comes to winning and keeping customers.

5. Let them know that you're thinking about them. Send your customers congratulatory cards for birthdays, promotions, graduations, or anything you can congratulate them for. Add a personal touch to relating with your customers (23).

EMPLOYEES AND CUSTOMER SERVICE

Michael LeBeouf believes, "how customers feel about the people that serve or sell them is a key factor in winning and keeping them" (22). A customer will tend to be loyal to any person who serves him satisfactorily, just as he will become disloyal to the person who serves him unsatisfactorily. This is why it is invaluable for employees to take the time to be nice to their customers. The attitude of employees, especially those who deal directly with the customers can either make or mar the business. Every employee should therefore endeavour to make good impression on the customers. For, it is the first impression made on a customer that determines whether the customer will come back for business or stay off. Also, management of organisations should endeavour to spell out to their employees that theirs are service-oriented business organisations. This will enable the frontline employees to know how to sell themselves to customers.

It is very important to note that customers don't often distinguish between the employees and the organisations they work for. As far as the customers are concerned, you are the company. This is the view of Kristin Anderson and Ron Zanke (24), which they further expatiate as follows: "In your one-to-one contact with customers, the once vague impersonal company takes on shape and substance." Therefore, they opine that "When your job involves serving customers and dealing with the public, how good a job you do with and for them ...determines how successful your company will be" Anderson and Zanke are strongly convinced that "In your hands, is the power to make that contact magical and memorable. In your hands is the power to keep customers coming back."

In other words, you alone can make or break the chain of great service.

Also in the opinion of Anderson and Zanke,

Some of the things you do to provide knock-your-socks-off service are relatively simple and easy, such as choosing your language carefully.

Other actions you take are more complex. Customers expect you to make the organisation to work for them. They expect you to understand the big picture and to be able to answer their questions, solve their problems, and refer them to just the right people for just the right things (24).

If an employee falls short of this expectation of customers, it means that both the employee and his company have failed in the perception of the customers, and they will tend to change to where they will likely get their problems solved.

On how to keep satisfying the needs and demands of customers, Anderson and Zanke (24) believe that the following questions will help to guide your personal service efforts:

1. What do my customers want from me, and from my company? Think both about what your customers need and what your customers expect.

2. How do support areas – e.g. billing or shipping – work to serve my customers? Consider your role in making the different areas of your company work in harmony for your customers.
3. What are the details – little things – that make a big difference in my customers' satisfaction?

Employees are to use the information that these questions provide to choose actions that will 'knock the socks off' the customers.

Still on the employee/customer relationship, Michael LeBeouf suggests three key-points in customer service, which are:

1. The most important goal of any employee, including salespersons, is to create and keep customers. LeBeouf believes that making sales creates short-term dollars, while creating customers makes long-and-short-term dollars.
2. There's a big difference between selling and helping people to buy. Helping people to buy takes an approach of 'let's find out what the customer wants or needs and see if we can match it with what we have. If we don't have it, maybe we can order it or make it. If not, let's send him to someone who can help serve him. Selling creates sales. Helping people to buy creates customers. And this latter attitude is far better than the former in today's business environment. This is because when we create and have customers, the sales will take care of themselves.

3. People love to buy, but hate to be sold. Also people love to own, to acquire, and yes, and to spend money. These make us feel important and successful. We gladly take all the credit for the purchase we are proudest of, but are quick to blame the seller when we feel short-changed. Therefore as an employee or a sales-person, endeavour to help people to buy; don't ever try to sell them.

As observed by Sunny Obazu-Ojeagbase (17), today,

> The market place is changing. No longer is it enough for you to focus on the cash your customer is bringing to your till without being genuinely concerned that what you sell to him is what he wants.

It is when you help the customer to buy what he wants that he derives joy and satisfaction from your service. And the more customers are satisfied with your product or service, the greater the probability of the survival of your business.

EVALUATING CUSTOMER SERVICE

Just how do customers evaluate the service they receive from business organisation? A Texas A and M Researcher, Dr. Leonard Benrry, observes that customers evaluate service on the basis of five factors:

1. Reliability – the ability to provide what was promised, dependably and accurately

2. Responsiveness – the willingness to help customers promptly.
3. Assurance – the knowledge and courtesy you show to customers, and your ability to convey trust, competence, and confidence.
4. Empathy – the degree of caring and individual attention you show customers.
5. Tangibles – the physical facilities and equipments, and your own (and others) appearance.

Kristin Anderson and Ron Zanke explain these five evaluative factors thus:

When you fulfil a customer order on time, you show reliability. When you notice a customer puzzling over a product and offer help and information, you show responsiveness. When you smile and tell a customer, "I can help you with that" – and do – you build assurance. When you are sensitive to an individual customer's needs when solving a problem, you show empathy. And when you take the time to make yourself and your work area presentable, you are paying attention to the tangibles. ("You are the Company" 24).

Anderson and Zanke observe,

Customers expectations of service organisations are loud and clear: look good, be responsive, be reassuring through courtesy and competence, be empathetic but, most of all, be reliable. Do what you said you would do. Keep the service of promise 24).

We can never over-state the fact that the business organisations and employees that are able to work towards satisfying these evaluative factors will no doubt have more than enough customers flocking round to do business with them, which will eventually lead them to swimming in the ocean of wealth as a result of increase in profit margin.

To Richard F. Gerson, "Customer service pays, it does not cost. It pays in many ways, the first of which is long-term customer retention" ("Developing Superior Customer Service Programme" 19). Also,

Good service makes management easier because everybody is committed to satisfying the customer. The results will be increased productivity and profits simply because management and employees are working to achieve the same goal (19).

Good customer service also enhances marketing. This is in the sense that it motivates customers to spread the good word about your service and business. In fact, the advantages of good customer service are inexhaustible.

And in a country like Nigeria where corruption and dishonesty seem to be reigning sway in the business world, the veteran motivational publisher, Sunny Obazu-Ojeagbase, believes,

Any business in Nigeria that decides to eliminate this practice of pocketing customers' money without giving a damn about what happened to the product they sold once the customer stepped out of the door will prosper more than those who don't. ("How Not to Woo Customers" 16).

The main reason for this is that the business environment in Nigeria is in dire need of business owners and employees who have the sincere desire to serve and help customers without short-changing them. Any individual or organisation that decides to fill this great gap will no doubt have a breakthrough to the world of wealth.

On the other hand a business that totally neglects customers' satisfaction will definitely suffer lack of patronage. This is mainly because customers want to derive maximum satisfaction from whatever they spend their hard-earned money on. To greedily and deviously plot to give less for the customers' precious money is to foolishly scare away your hard-won customers. It is, in a way, being penny wise and pound foolish.

THE COST OF LOSING A CUSTOMER

Figure out how much it costs to lose a customer. Richard F. Gerson reveals a formula for doing this. Based on information from the U.S. Office of Consumer Affairs, the formula requires the knowledge of three figures to be complete: your annual revenues, the number of customers you have and your cost of acquiring and keeping them, including marketing, sales, advertising, promotion, discounts, etc. ("Developing Superior

Customer Service Programme" 19). And to Magnus Abeng,

The cost of losing a customer is, among others, 'in pre-investment cost which is the cost you incur before you get the customers to patronize you ...It also takes personal selling, advertisement, good behaviour and other promotional strategies to turn them from onlookers to customers ("The Cost of Losing A Customer" 24).

In fact Richard Gerson believes that it costs five to six times more to acquire a customer than it does to do business with a current or former customer. And to lose such a customer after you have spent so much to acquire him is, in fact, an unquantifiable loss.

And there is even more to the cost of losing a customer than all that have been stated above.

Another component of loses is that the time and investment that you have lost on the customer that is gone, and which you are trying to woo back could actually have been used in gaining new customers (Magnus Abeng, 24).

This means a double loss in the sense that the amount of money and time you would have used to acquire additional customers is used to substitute or bring back lost ones. In a way, you have not really replaced or won back the lost customers, even if you succeed in bringing them back. What you have done is simply digging a pit and pouring your hard-earned resources into it. Also, you are denying yourself the opportunity of further promoting your business and winning new customers when you spend all your time and resources running after run-away customers. The consequence of this is that you will continue to turn around on the same spot or deteriorate into oblivion. It costs much to lose customers.

Another cost of losing a customer is the revenue lost between the time the customer stopped doing business from your organisation and when he is brought back. Within this period your organisation would, no doubt, have spent some money, time and resources in the day-to-day running of the business without a meaningful corresponding income due to run-away customers.

As observed by Magnus Abeng,

Another indeterminable cost of losing a customer is the cost that will result from the stories your customer would have told your other customers about you and your company and the reason for their stopping to do business with you (24).

This consequence is, in fact, the greatest among the various costs of losing a customer. This is because it has the capability of running down your business to the point of closure. In fact, it is because of this cost that

Researchers have revealed that for every customer you lost, there is the tendency that you will soon lose ten other ones or, in the same vein, for every complaint from customers, there are ten outside there with complaints but who wouldn't relay them to you. So when one leaves, he tells others and others tell yet others and the evil flame burns like wild fire and your business is as good as dead! So a lost customer could mean losing the entire customers (Magnus Abeng, 24).

The only way to avoid this kind of ugly experience is to put in place a standard for optimum customer satisfaction and a service-oriented policy so that no customer will have a cause to walk out of your business premises to tell any ugly story about you, your product and your service. Endeavour to make every customer that comes your way satisfied so that when he goes out there, he will have only the story of your superior products and services to tell others. This, indeed, is the good news that will make customers to continuously flood your business premises, remain loyal and make your profit margin to increase tremendously.

TOWARDS RECOVERING LOST CUSTOMERS

If, for one reason or the other, you have lost so many customers and you are interested in bringing them back, what do you have to do? Before you think of doing anything to bring back your run-away customers, you must, first of all, identify what made them to stop doing business with you or your organisation in the first place.

The reason might be as a result of any of the following, as suggested by Richard F. Gerson (20):

1. Uncaring employees;
2. Negative attitude of employees toward customers;
3. Poor employee training;
4. Differences in perception between what businesses think customers want and what customers actually want;
5. Differences in perception between the way businesses think customers want to be treated and the way customers really want to be treated, or are actually treated;
6. Differences in perception between the product or service businesses think they provide and what customers think they receive;
7. No customer service philosophy within the company;
8. Poor handling and resolution of complaints;
9. Employees are not empowered to provide good service, take responsibility and make decisions that will satisfy the customer;
10. Poor treatment of employees as customers

It is particularly necessary that you first identify the cause before you think of the remedy. Or else, you might just be chasing shadows or wasting your precious resources on expensive advertisement campaigns that will be seen by your aggrieved run-away customers as mere propaganda, and that will yield no positive results.

Kathryn Clark, a contributor to Small Business Opportunities, gives some tips on ways to draw back lost customers:

1. Give your old customers a little attention – attend to their complaints;
2. All they might need is a little encouragement. You need to let them know that you sincerely care about the loss of their business;
3. Produce a practical sales letter that seeks to recover these valuable lost clients. Thank them for past orders and make them to know that they are greatly missed. A light and humorous approach can be effective. The approach should also be casual and friendly;
4. Try to rekindle their purchasing process with your company
(From Femi Olasusi's "Recovering Your Lost Customers" 26-27).

B.I. Oladejo, Managing Director, Goodwill Investment and Marketing Company Limited, also provides some formulae for winning back run-away customers:

1. Customer Forum – where customers (the lost ones) will ask questions and their grievances will be addressed;
2. Give Incentives – by contacting or writing them, apologizing for wrongs done them and offering a price out with other affordable incentives;

3. Home Delivery - by luring them with such facilities as offsetting the cost of delivery
(From Femi Olasusi's "Recovering Your Lost Customers" 26).

For Andem Effiong, a Chief Consultant with the Centre for Management Development, Lagos, what need to be done to win back lost customers include:

1. Persuasion – persuading the lost customers to give you and your company another chance;
2. Public Relations – especially involvement in community activities; and
3. Additional Incentives – like bulk breaking, repackaging, discounts, home/office delivery, etc.
(From Femi Olasusi's "Recovering Your Lost Customers" 27).

The strategies to be adopted for recovering lost customers can in no way be discussed exhaustively in any single text. And, as we have pointed out earlier, the best approach is to identify the cause(s) of customers' disloyalty in order to undertake the most appropriate remedy. However, in most cases, you may have to make another investment entirely in time and other resources in order to woo your lost customers. But, however great may be the cost of bringing back your old customers, the long-term benefits it will bring to your company can, in no way, be quantified in terms of increased profits and continuous loyalty of customers that will accrue to your company.

DESIGNING A CUSTOMER RETENTION PROGRAMME

As observed by Richard F. Gerson (20),

Customers today are better educated than ever before. They are more careful about their purchases and the dollars they spend. They want value for their money. They also want good service and they are willing to pay for it.

Entrepreneurs and their employees are therefore to ensure that they do not only endeavour to recover their lost customers, but also design and adopt such customer services that will help them in retaining their customers as they come patronizing.

The number one thing to consider in the issue of customer retention is the quality of products or services being offered. It is an obvious fact that no customer will want to remain with any company or business organisation that offers sub-standard or inferior goods or services. Every business owner must therefore take care of the quality of his products or services, since this is what determines whether he will stay long in business. This issue is one that needs to be urgently addressed by Nigerian businessmen and women, some of who take delight in offering sub-standard, inferior or even fake products to customers. Luckily for Nigeria's business world, the Government has set up an agency, NAFDAC that is saddled with the task of ensuring the quality of products that are brought into the Nigerian market for consumers. And, from all indications, this agency is very much equal to the task.

In the view of Magnus Abeng (24),

The solution to customer retention... is a systematic decision by the organisation on whether they are going to be customer-oriented or not... The organisation should be involved and interested in customer relation as well as surpassing their customer satisfaction.

What Abeng is understood to be saying here is that the management of an organisation should make a foremost decision to be customer-oriented. It is when this decision is made and channelled across and down the entire organisation that employees' actions and inactions, activities and inactivities will be in line with the management's customer service policy. It is this policy decision that will even determine the quality of products or services that are offered to customers.

Another strategy to be adopted in order to ensure customer retention, according to Magnus Abeng, is to take care of internal customers. These are the different departments of the organization that relate with each other in the process of producing a product. Abeng believes that each of these departments has some expectations from both themselves and the organisation which, if not satisfied, can immediately be translated to the faces of employees who might unavoidably pass it on the innocent external customers and cause them to stay away from the organisation. Thus the solution here is for management to make sure that both the external customers and internal customers are taken care of. When internal customers (workers) are satisfied with management, it becomes quite easy to satisfy external customers (buyers).

One other thing in the issue of customer retention is that of pricing. Richard F. Gerson observes that "Shoppers are price conscious. They often switch brands or business suppliers simply because one provides a price advantage over the other" (20). To prevent this, business owners are not only to make sure that they are not at a disadvantage in pricing, but also to endeavour to provide superior customer service, as well as employ various customer retention strategies such as establishing a personal relationship with the customers. The focus is to make it hard for customers to leave you for your competitors. Under no condition must you allow the customers' loyalty that has been established to break. And if it becomes necessary, please pet your customers, they deserve it.

Remember that people are loyal to a business because they feel they are treated well, they receive good value for their money, and they are psychologically or physically attached to the business (Richard F. Gerson, "Developing Superior Customer Service Programmes" 20).

In the opinion of Femi Olasusi, "Few people will maintain a bad view of your company when you are genuinely concerned about your possible deficiencies and are eager to resolve any issue" (Recovering Your Lost Customers" 27). And the motivational publisher, Sunny Obazu-Ojeagbase, attempts a fore-cast of the survival of business organisations in the very near future: "In years to come, your business survival will depend on how many customers you can bring back after making the first initial sales to them" ("How Not to Woo Customers" 17).

To push the issue of customer retention and business survival to an elusive future date can be seen as being unrealistic in the face of the prevalent economic reality. Contrary to the future gaze of Obazu-Ojeagbase, business survival, today, is dependent on how many customers business owners and their employees can bring back after the initial business contact. This is more so considering the increasing scarcity and continuous devaluation of financial resources in the hands of consumers, as well as the fierce competition among the various business organisations.

To prove that the issues of customer retention and business survival are matters of the moment, let me recount an experience that I had some years ago. I wanted to do my business letterheads, business cards and staff identity cards. I personally designed sketches of these items and took them to a computer centre so that they will help design and print them out with the computer. Unfortunately for me, I attached as a sample the business card of a former course mate who I recently ran into, and who told me to try as much as possible to contact him for some business connections.

After agreeing on the amount I was to pay, I was told to come for the completed job in two day's time. According to them they were busy with some jobs that they could not do mine immediately. Well, I agreed. And on the third day I went back for the job, only to discover that they had not made any attempt to do my job because they could not even remember that I gave them any job.

It took me quite some agonizing time and explanation to bring to the remembrance of the man-in-charge that I did give them the job of designing a letterhead, a business card and an identity card. When, at last, he was convinced that I actually gave them the job, he started searching for the sketches of the job that I gave to them. He searched through files, through piles of documents, under tables and gadgets; he ransacked everywhere, including their waste bins. But lo and behold, my papers were nowhere to be found!

I was enraged. I couldn't believe that the letterheads, business cards and staff identity cards that took me so much effort, imagination and time to sketch out had been thrown away in such a careless way. Then I remembered my friend's complimentary card that I attached to the job as sample. My God! I had not even taken down the contact address, neither had I been able to contact my friend for the promised business connection. I was mad with anger! I thundered at them with rage. But all I could receive from them were feeble apologies and empty promises to handle my job with care and speed if I could give them another sketch.

Well, there was nothing I could do. It was painful that I had again lost contact with my friend. Obviously, my hope of making some very powerful business connection with my friend who worked with a brokerage firm at Port Harcourt had, carelessly, slipped away. But what do I do? I still needed the letterheads, business cards and identity cards. I had no option than to give them another chance. Therefore I took the pains to sketch out these items again and took them to the same Computer Centre the following day. At least, I wanted them to vindicate their promises, and to at least be opportune to right the wrong they had done.

This time, they agreed to reduce the price by giving me 20|% discount. Good. And they asked me to collect the completed job the following day. Another pass mark for improved speed! The wounds they had inflicted in my spirit were beginning to receive some healing balm.

And it was in that recuperating condition and with renewed great expectation that my job would be ready for collection that I got to the Computer Centre the following day.

But, can you imagine? My job had not been done. They were still trying to complete some other urgent jobs. Again, apologies and promises. I was told to come the following day. The following day, I was there. They had managed to type some few lines of my job into the computer, but had to abandon it to finish off the other urgent jobs. Meanwhile, it was already weekend; therefore I had to come the following week.

The following week, they tried to do my job, but could not finish it. Apologies and promises. The third week they fed everything into the computer, but could not get around to printing it. Apologies and promises. The fourth week, they wanted to print but the printer had some faults and they were taking it for repairs. Apologies and promises. The fifth week, the printer had been repaired but ink got finished. Apologies and promises. The sixth week, they could buy only black ink, but did not see coloured ink to buy. Apologies and promises. The seventh week, the condition was still the same. I was frustrated.

I decided not to call back for a period of three weeks. But when I got back after a period of almost a month, can you believe it? They had not been able to buy coloured ink, and my job was still trapped in their computer. I was fed up. I decided to abandon them and the job. I re-sketched my job, boarded a vehicle to Warri, and gave the job to another Computer/Business Centre.

I got there some minutes past eight in the morning; we agreed on the price which, surprisingly, was even lower than that of the ill-fated Computer Centre at Abraka. I gave them the job and I was told to come back around 11 o'clock. About some minutes after eleven, I got back to see that they had not only finished feeding the job into the computer, but that they had even printed out the drafts of the job and they were waiting for me to come and read through and correct any errors. Greatly impressed, I quickly proof-read the drafts, highlighted the few errors and handed back the drafts to them.

And, before I could settle down to glance through the newspapers that were provided for waiting customers, surprisingly, they had finished correcting the errors and had printed out my job, precisely to my specification and taste. I was not only satisfied, but I was highly impressed. What one Computer Centre could not do within the period of three months, another Computer Centre had done it within three hours! It was more than Seven-Up, the difference was clear!

Now, supposing I have another job to do next time, where do you think I will go! Or, if any of my friends wants to do some job with the Computer, Where do you think I will recommend to them? Your guess is as good as mine. And this is one of the invaluable advantages of good customer service.

LASTLINE

So far in this chapter, we have been able to dwell on the greatest secret of business success. It is an open secret which has been neglected by so many business owners of today. But the few business owners who have, over the ages, adopted this great secret in their business relation with their customers have, no doubt, reaped great benefits and rewards from it.

The secret has been thrown open before all. Peradventure you have not been able to grasp it up till this moment, the secret is: Recognise and worship the customer as the king of your business. If you are able to do this and satisfy every of your customers through your good customer service, the sky will not just be the limit, but indeed the stepping stone to your great, astounding and outstanding achievements in the business world.

10

3 Cornerstones for Building Great Wealth

Through wisdom is an house builded; and by understanding it is established. And by knowledge shall the chambers be filled with all precious and pleasant riches.
- Proverbs 24: 2-3

They are always together – the three infallible catalysts. They are almost inseparable. They go hand-in-hand, with their almost omnipotent ability to effect action and bring things into existence. We are talking about nothing else but the trio of wisdom, knowledge and understanding. A furtive look at the above quotation from the book of Proverbs should confirm to us the creative potency of these three friends. It tells us, without mincing words, that no house can be built, unless through wisdom and that every house is established only by understanding; and, by the time the house is finally completed, it takes knowledge to fill its chambers with all precious and pleasant riches. But, what is responsible for the great creative ability of these three virtues/concepts? Let us begin with wisdom.

Wisdom

Otherwise referred to as the principal thing, wisdom is obviously the most potent, after God, of all creative forces. Wisdom is, without doubt, at the centre of all creative actions in the human society. Without it, nothing of importance will happen or spring forth in humanity. The primary reason for this is that with wisdom comes strength (Proverbs 24: 5).

What then is wisdom? Authorities have continued to see wisdom as nothing but correct application of knowledge, particularly in relation to solving human problems. Knowledge, on its own, is the acquisition of relevant information that could be used to solve human problems. This is to say that knowledge provides the raw materials with which wisdom works towards solving man's problems. Hence, continuous acquisition of knowledge increases the strength (physical and mental) that a man would need for tackling his problems. And, in the final analysis, when the knowledge is aptly applied and the problems are solved, this man of wisdom emerges stronger than ever, and is fully programmed to face greater challenges (Proverbs 24:5).

In Proverbs 4:7, the wise king, after trying his hand on virtually everything under the sun, concludes, "Wisdom is the principal thing". This is probably because, without any amount of wisdom, it is doubtful whether a person will survive in this life. Yes, we need wisdom to stay alive. It is wisdom that will direct you on where to go and where not to go; what to do and what not to do; how to talk and how not to talk; what to look at and what not to look at; what to hear and what not to hear; how to do things and how not to do things; how to live and how not to live, etc. Without wisdom, it is obvious that a person will always get himself into trouble.

As we talk about the secret of building great and lasting wealth, one basic thing that guarantees success is the ability to do things intelligently. It is important to note that the kind of things you do, the way you do them, the time you do them and the place at which you do them matter a lot. For one reason, it is not everything that you do that brings you success and prosperity. Rather, some things will bring you success and prosperity, while some others will bring you failure and poverty. This is the reason why we need to be careful in selecting the things we do. There are wrong things and there are right things; there are wrong ways of doing things and there are right ways of doing things; there are wrong places for doing particular things and there are right places for doing particular things. It therefore behooves the man of wisdom to do the right things in the right ways at the right time and at the right places. This is how to do things intelligently, and it takes wisdom to be able to do that.

But the ready question to ask at this point is, "How do you know the right thing to do, the right way to do it, the right time to do it and the right place at which to do it? Well, the rightness or wrongness of things is relative, and is dependent on individual perception. What I regard as right may be seen as wrong by another person, and vice versa. The issue of regarding something as right or wrong is subjective. However, in our societies, there are acceptable norms and values which, if negated, would be seen as wrong. For instance, it is wrong in some societies for a woman to wear trousers, while in some other societies, it is acceptable. The rightness or wrongness of things, here, is dependent on societal norms and values.

To a great extent, the values that society places on things are congruent with established principles of living. To form the habit of doing things that society regards as wrong will most probably lead you into trouble and failure, while doing things that society approves as right will most probably lead you out of trouble , and into success and prosperity.

Nevertheless, the rightness or wrongness of the things you do, more importantly, depends on the targets or goals that you have set for yourself. In this wise, society does not have much to say in the rightness or wrongness of the things you do. For example, a man who has set the goal of building an empire of wealth, but spends every kobo that comes his way without considering the need to set aside some percentage of his income for the purpose of wealth-building is surely doing the wrong thing. Obviously, to society, he may not be doing wrong by spending his own money; or he may not even be doing wrong things with the money. But as long as what he is doing negates his goal, then it is wrong. The question that you must ask yourself here is, "what is my goal or target in life?" After you have answered this important question, then you must check whether you are doing things in pursuance of that goal.

This is where you will know whether you are doing the wrong things or the right things. If the things you are doing are not related to your set goal, then you are doing the wrong things. And such things can delay or hinder you from reaching your goal. On the other hand, if the things you are doing are related to your set goals, then you are doing the right things; and such things can lead you to or quicken your journey towards your goals.

It is only when you do the right things that you can get the right results.

But it is one thing to do the right things, it is quite another to do the things right. This is in the sense that it is possible to do the right things in the wrong way. Thus, how you do things matters a lot. To habitually do things foolishly or haphazardly can either delay or hinder you from reaching your goal. And to be outstanding in any area of human endeavor, you must not only do whatever you do with all your might, you must also do it intelligently. This is where wisdom comes in. To do things intelligently is to make sure not to do things 'any how'; it is taking time to do things carefully, meticulously, correctly, precisely and accurately. Also, to do things intelligently is to do things at the right time, at the right place, in the right way or manner, and for the right purpose. As we have just hinted above, wisdom is the guiding spirit that enables us to do things intelligently. Do you have it? Think about it!

As we talk about the need to do the right things at the right time, we are naturally brought to the issue of allocating time to the things that we have to do. And on this point, the Preacher, in Ecclesiastes 3:1-8, reminds us that there is time for everything and every purpose under heaven. This is to say, there is nothing you want to do here on earth that you cannot find time to do. However great or enormous that thing may be, you will always find time enough to do it. All it takes is your ability to appropriately allocate time to it. People like Shakespeare wrote volumes of books because they allocated time to writing. And many other people have done and continue to do great and spectacular things because of adequate allocation of time to whatever they have to do in order to realize their goals. How then are you allocating time to the things that you have to do in order to reach your goal?

One of the greatest and saddest tragedies of life is that we, human beings, have continued to murder time. Consequently, we do not always have time enough to do the important things that we ought to do. For those who do not know, time is un-debatably the most valuable asset on earth. Whatever else you have; if you do not have time, then you do not have anything. This is because, with time comes everything; or everything comes with time. When a person dies, what simply happens is that the person has come to the end of his time on earth; he has no more time to live. And when there is no more time like that, that person can no longer do anything. For him, time has ended. And with this sudden end of time often comes the realities of wasted time. It is at the point of death that man often realizes that there are so many things that he ought to have done but which he did not do. This belated realization often makes so many people to die regretfully and painfully.

It is so that you and I will not regret at the point of death that I am writing these words to stir you into action. Time here on earth is very brief, and it will soon pass. Within this short time of our existence here on earth, there are so many things we ought to do. And unless we wisely allocate our time to everything that needs to be done, we will continue to rob Peter to pay Paul, and we will end up accomplishing very little. For some other people, they develop the habit of perpetually struggling to kill time just when things are getting out of hands. If you find yourself in this category, remember this: he who murders sleep sleeps no more. In the same way, he who kills time has no time enough to do what he ought to do. Be wise, do the right things at the right time, and you will have no need to kill time.

It is agreed that Rome was not built in a day. But it is equally true that it did not take eternity to build Rome. Rome was eventually built because the Romans took time to do the things that needed to be done. You cannot build your empire of wealth in one day. But you do not have eternity within which to build it. You have just a short time to live. And you must do everything you ought to do within this short period of your existence. What then are the things that you ought to do in order to succeed in life, or in order to build you empire of wealth? Are you doing them now? If not, why not? Be wise; wake up and work. And as you go about doing the right things (that you ought to do) make sure you do the things right in order to get the right results.

After all has been said and done, Solomon, the wise king, exhorts us all to get wisdom; because there is nothing that is better than wisdom. The question then is, "How do I get wisdom?" The human tendency here is to presume that wisdom, being regarded by man as common sense, is common to all. But the truth is, wisdom is a scarce commodity within the human race. This is responsible for the countless foolish things that are done by men and women, and even nations, all over the world. Also, when we talk about the need to get wisdom, the tendency is that you will look at yourself and think that you already have it. But, however great the amount of wisdom you claim to possess, God sees all as nothing but foolishness and self-conceit. And to be wise in your own eyes is very dangerous. It leads only to destruction and ruin. You can go and confirm that from people like

Pharaoh, Goliath, Nebuchadnezzar, Herod, Judas Iscariot, Ananias and Sapphira, just to mention a few. Yes, human wisdom is rubbish; worldly wisdom is devilish; but Godly wisdom is profitable. If you have it, you will have all the good things of life. But how do you get it?

Job 28:12-13 says that wisdom is not found in the land of the living. You can get it only from God. The wisdom that comes from God is like the one that God gave to Bezaleel in Exodus 31:2-3, "See I have called by name Bezaleel the son of Uri, the son of Hur, of the tribe of Judah: And I have filled him with the spirit of God, in wisdom, and in understanding, and in knowledge, and in all manner of workmanship." It is also the kind of wisdom that God gave to Solomon in 1 King 3:12, "Behold, I have done according to thy words: lo, I have given thee a wise and understanding heart; so that there was none like thee before thee, neither after thee shall any rise like unto thee" and in 1 King 4:29, "And God gave Solomon wisdom and understanding exceeding much and largeness of heart, even as the sand that is on the sea shore. And Solomon's wisdom excelled the wisdom of all the children of the east country, and all the wisdom of Egypt. For he was wiser than all men." Yes, as in 1 Chronicles 22:12, "Only the Lord (can) give thee wisdom and understanding." He gave it to Moses, Joseph, Bezaleel, Solomon, Ezra, Daniel, Peter, Stephen, Paul, and Jesus Christ himself is the 'Wisdom' of God personified.

In the same way, God can give you this kind of wisdom. All you need to do is to, first of all, acknowledge your lack of wisdom, to seek for it with all your heart, and by asking God for it as is commanded in

James 1:5: "If any of you lack wisdom, let him ask of God, that giveth to all men liberally, and upbraideth not; and it shall be given him." And you must have the faith that when you ask God for wisdom, He will give it to you.

When wisdom begins to come, it starts with the fear of God, then to having the knowledge of God, and then to understanding the things of the Spirit of God. This wisdom seeks to make peace with God and with all men, and to live a quiet life. The wisdom is also profitable and strengthens all those who have it to do exploit. There is no good thing on earth that you cannot get with wisdom. "Happy is the man that findeth wisdom." Have you found it? Think about it!

Understanding

Another of the three cornerstones for building great and lasting wealth is, understanding. Proverbs 24: 2-3 holds that a house is built through wisdom, but it takes understanding to establish it. What this simply means is that, for knowledge to function as a useful raw material, it must be understood. The knowledge that is not understood can build only a poor structure if used as a raw material. Therefore whatever knowledge you are acquiring for the building of your life, destiny, career and wealth, please take time to study, analyze and understand it thoroughly. Be sure that it is suitable for your kind of building before using it. When this is done, your structure is sure to be well established.

Your success in life depends largely on your level of understanding. Life is such an intricate phenomenon that to succeed in life, you must, first of all, understand the intricacies of life. Failure to do this is to get yourself perplexed in the complexity of the labyrinths of life.

As you labour to succeed in life, the first thing you must do is to observe and understand the natural principles of life. God has created the world in such a way that everything has its own time and season. You are therefore expected to study this natural order of things and events so that you can do things at their appropriate time.

Clearly related to this is the need for you to understand the cycles, trends and fashions of things. It is a common knowledge that life is dynamic. Events and things in life do not stand still, but they keep changing. And a person who has the desire to succeed in life will take it upon himself to study and understand the trends, cycles, fashions of things and the direction of events around him. People like Bill Gates and Steve Jobs were able to study, understand and have visions of the direction of the evolving computer technology, and they were and are still able to make fortunes out of that. You can duplicate what Bill Gates or Steve Jobs has done by trying to understand the trend and direction of events and technological changes so that you can adequately position yourself for success in the near future.

In my classical blueprint for wealth building, *Steps for Building an Empire of Wealth,* I wrote on the need for you to get acquainted with the secrets of success. There, I pointed out that life is a game, and that you cannot play the game successfully unless you understand the modus operandi for playing the game. Yes, there are general principles and particular secrets of success which you must learn and apply before you can succeed. These principles and secrets are invaluable and greatly needed for building a worthwhile life and making significant success and progress in life's endeavours. Failure to get hold of these secrets is the reason why you will continue to swim in the ocean of failure and defeat.

How do you get the secrets? You can get the secrets of success from other people. There are thousands, f not millions, of people who have lived successfully virtually in all areas of human endeavours. These people did some specific things that made them to succeed. Try to find out those things which gave them success; study them thoroughly; understand them clearly; try to do or repeat those things which they did in exactly the same way; and you will be surprised by the similarity or sameness of the result that will come out. This is not an attempt to play gimmicks on you; rather, it is a fact of life which you need to try out.

I guess your next question is about how to have access to the experiences of and the secrets employed by others. Very simple and very easy. You can get all you need to know – all the secrets you need for success – from books, books and books. Just about two or three decades ago, a young American undergraduate got frustrated and dropped out of the renowned Harvard University. Then, I suppose the people around him would have regarded him as an abysmal failure. But just after that, this young man had access to an American magazine, *Popular Electronics* and got introduced to the then emergent computer technology. He sought more information on this new technology from books, magazines, periodicals and other information sources, and eventually came out with a vision of a future with a computer on every desk using his own operating system. He went to work on that vision and, today, he is ranked as the richest man in the world, netting well above $33 million daily.

What is the initial source of Bill Gates' outstanding success? INFORMATION! How did he get his information? From books, magazines and periodicals. How did they get there? They are the records of other people's knowledge, experiences and research findings – all these are the secrets which Bill Gates gathered, organized and applied for his own success. Why not go ahead and do the same thing? After all, the books, magazines, periodicals and all the present-day sophisticated information materials are there for your use. Go ahead and get the secrets of success from them.

God expects that man benefits immensely from his environment. That is why He took time to create everything that man needs for his survival in the first place. To fail to take advantage of the abundant resources in your environment is to cheat yourself of the blessings that are meant for you. Most of the resources that are prevalent in your environment take the form of natural, material and human resources. You are expected to study, understand and find ways of organizing these available resources for your survival.

Particularly, the natural and the material resources in your environment are very good sources of financial resources. To a very large extent, your survival and success in life depends on your ability to exploit, organize and convert these natural and material resources to cash. To help you in this bid are the human resources, which, if effectively employed, can guarantee you a life of abundance. The starting point therefore is to understand these basic resources and the various ways in which they can be combined for profitable use.

Another reason why you need to understand your environment is so as to isolate the opportunities available for exploitation. In all the human societies in the world, there are myriads of human needs that ought to be satisfied. The very fact that human beings are insatiable is the reason why there are always gaps of human needs yet to be filled in our societies. A man who has an eagle eye for opportunities will therefore try as much as possible to study and understand his environment in relation to the needs of the people within the environment. This is with the intent of isolating such human needs which are yet to be satisfied within the society or community. If he is able to do this, he then finds ways of providing those services or products which are lacking in the society. This, in fact, is the highway to wealth and to great accomplishment.

As you study and try to understand your environment and the people in your community, you also need to study and understand you own self. If you don't know it, you are a special specie and a peculiar person in the universe. In the whole of this wide, wild world, there is no other person that is exactly like you. You must know that you are fearfully and wonderfully made for a particular purpose. Your existence here on earth at this particular time and place is not by accident. It is in accordance with the ordained plan of God. You are here to fulfill a particular purpose or mission for humanity. And God is counting on you and you only, for its fulfillment. You must therefore try as much as possible to understand youself, and to identify the purpose or mission for which you are here.

God has put within you all that you need for the fulfillment of your purpose; and you have no reason to fail. Thus, the starting point is for you to study yourself thoroughly with the intention of identifying those peculiar qualities which are meant to help you in fulfilling your mission. These qualities often take the form of special talents, skills and natural abilities, and they go a long way to reflect what you can do to contribute to the growth and progress of the human society. In other words, our mission or purpose on earth cannot be far from your innate potentials, talents, skills and natural abilities. It is from these that you determine what mission God has equipped you to perform.

Naturally, your identified mission on earth should specify the job or task you should be engaged in. This is the area where very many people are missing it. Most often, very many people, because of their immediate need for survival or because of the fear of venturing into the unknown, find themselves doing the wrong things or are in the wrong places. This is the reason why very many people in the world are unfulfilled in life. For you to live a fulfilled life and die a satisfied man, you must engage in those tasks or jobs that have to do with your identified mission or purpose on earth.

When eventually you find yourself faced with such jobs or tasks that will lead you to fulfilling your mission, you should try as much as possible to understand them. In the first place, what are you expected to do, and how do you go about doing them? Learn all you need to know about the job or task. And you need to be informed that the know-how for doing virtually every kind of job or task is contained in books. Tucked somewhere on the shelf of a library or bookshop is a book that can teach you all you need to know about your job or the task at hand. All you need to do is to develop the habit of avid reading. If you can get into this habit, you will not only improve tremendously on your stock of vital information and general knowledge which will give you a better understanding of your job or task, but before long, you will become an authority in your field.

No doubt, we have seen the great importance of understanding and the role it plays in our pursuit of success and prosperity in life. We have seen that understanding does not only make it easier for us to get our means of livelihood or sustenance, but that it creates the way for us to achieve greatness as well as to fulfill our missions on earth. No wonder the Bible, in Proverbs 3:13, declares blessedness on the person who is able to get understanding. This is basically because understanding has the ability to sustain and keep us alive, as is confirmed in Proverbs 2:11. Thus the counsel for all is to endeavor to get understanding – to understand life and the principles of life; to understand the natural laws and secrets of success; to understand your environment and the needs of the people in your community; to understand yourself and your mission on earth; to understand your job and the task before you; to understand your world and how you can contribute towards its development; and to understand your God and how you can serve and please Him. When you are able to understand all these, there is no doubt that you will live successfully, happily, and eventually leave this world a fulfilled man.

Knowledge

Having built and established our house, it is time to fill it with state-of-the-art decorations and furniture. To effectively do this, knowledge becomes very handy. Our referred scripture holds that it is by knowledge that the chambers shall be filled with all precious and pleasant riches. And it is probably on the basis of this that Brian Tracy is so confident about the potency of knowledge, and strongly opines that "Power, position, influence and prestige tend to gravitate towards the person who acquires and then uses his or her knowledge the most effectively for the benefit of all." In other words, knowledge gives power, wealth and all that go with them. But, please note that it is not the man who acquires knowledge that commands power, position, influence, prestige and all the wealth and riches of life, but the one who uses his acquired knowledge for the benefit of humanity. This goes to say that acquisition of knowledge is not an end in itself, but a means to an end.

People say, "Knowledge is power", and God confirms it; for, He says, "My people are destroyed for lack of knowledge." That is to say, because God's people lacked knowledge, they had no power to fight back; hence they were destroyed by their enemies.

On the contrary, the veteran motivational writer, Napoleon Hill, is of the opinion that, knowledge is not power, but is only potential power. In his own view, knowledge "becomes power only when and if it is organized into definite plans of action and directed to a definite end." Well, Napoleon Hill's analytical view of knowledge is probably as good as God's own because, whether knowledge is power or potential power, the important thing is that it eventually becomes power or a source of power. And this is why we cannot but include it among the important principles of success and prosperity.

For now, let us be contented that knowledge is power, especially for those who will take the pains to organize it for practical use; or for those who will endeavor to acquire specialized knowledge. Yes, knowledge is power, because it is with the aid of knowledge that we can fight with and overcome many of the complicated and unyielding realities of life.

Let us consider, for instance, somebody who is a stark illiterate – one who does not know his left from his right – such a person will definitely commit a lot of blunders in the midst of our present-day civilized society. Of course, it is possible that such a person may, one way or the other, manage to get rich. But the embarrassment that he receives every now and then as he ignorantly steps on people's toes, or as he constantly struggles through communication barriers, especially with the prevalent foreign lingua franca, is, no doubt, enough to give him a cardiac heart arrest (CHA). And this is beside the sense of inferiority complex that perpetually plagues him; not even to talk of the many golden opportunities that he misses as a result of his inability to see or spot them out due to his stark illiteracy. No, illiteracy, really, is a disease, and it must be cured.

But in attempting to cure illiteracy, it is better not to cure it half-way. This is because, as they say, half education is dangerous. I wonder why they say so. After all, are they not the same people who also say that in the country of the blind, the one-eyed man is the king? That is true. But I think they say half education is dangerous because of the frustrations and regrets that result from unrealized dreams and squashed hopes of the partially educated man.

This reminds me of an old man I encountered in the hay days of the UPN/NPN political encounter. Worn with age and poverty-stricken, the hungry-looking old man, in tatters, stood by the eaves of his dilapidated hut watching. He was watching, dismayed, as the campaign team of one of Nigeria's greatest political figures meandered through the crowded street. The deafening shrieks of sirens and the confusing chants of "Up Awo!" "Up Nigeria!" "One Nation!" etc, rent the air. Curiosity had also brought me out to see with my eyes the pomp and pageantry of this deified political figure.

As I stood there, close to the old man, I was amazed at the overwhelming support and acclaim that this man possessed. I peeped through the shoulders of the crowd, and I saw him, balanced in the mercuric black Mercedes Benz. I saw his round-rimmed pair of glasses, his cap and the sweet fatherly smile. He was, as usual, waiving his 'V' sign to the supportive crowd. What a man!

After his train had passed, the crowd had thinned down and I had returned to myself, I realized that there was a feeble hand lightly resting on my shoulder. I turned, and I saw the wrinkled face of the old man. I saw his set of penetrating and bleary eyes.

"My son", he spoke with a shaky voice, but with a surprisingly fine accent of the Queen's English.

"My son, do you know that this Awolowo that has just passed was my classmate?"

"Is that true, Papa?" I couldn't help but be interested in what that old and poverty-ridden man was saying.

"Yes, he was my classmate, and he was not even as brilliant as me. I only had the misfortune of not completing my schooling when I lost my father. If not, I would have become somebody like that too."

As the old man spoke, I could see the streaks of regret, frustration and fury, all combined, in the old man's face. The tears in his bleary eyes were even beginning to drop freely. I wanted to say something to console the old man, but I found that I could not find my voice. Instead, I saw that I was also beginning to shed tears along with the old man. All I could do was just to pat the old man at the back sympathetically and ran back to my house, wagging my head. But there and then, I made up my mind that, whatever may happen, I was not going to have half education in my life.

Yes, half education is dangerous and should be avoided in order to avoid regrets, frustrations, bitterness and fury that result from unrealized dreams and quashed hopes.

This brings us to the need to have a good and thorough education. In Nigeria today, it is good and necessary for a person to have, at least, secondary school education, even if he is to learn a trade. This secondary school education will, no doubt, equip him to function well in the present day civilized Nigerian society. Gone are the days when children were forced to learn trades without any opportunity for acquiring formal education. Today, you either know some amount of A,B,C; 1,2,3 and can, at least answer the question, "Wetin you carry?" or you perish.

For those who, like me, were so obsessed by the desire to acquire good education, and so, could not learn any trade, I have this to say; rather, it is not I, but Glenn Bland who has this to say, "Education does not guarantee success and prosperity; only application of education will do that. In this era of mass unemployment, where millions of graduates are parading the streets, brandishing an assortment of certificates for non-existent jobs, it is only those who are able to apply the education that they have acquired over the years that will survive.

There is no gain-saying this fact, since certificates alone will not be able to secure you your meal tickets or guarantee you your means of livelihood.

Therefore all graduates and potential graduates should begin to look inward and assess the knowledge they have acquired over the years and see how they can organize and apply it for profitable use. And talking about assessing our knowledge for profitable use, we should be reminded that knowledge, as both Napoleon Hill and Glen Bland have observed, is divided into two kinds: generalized knowledge and specialized knowledge. With generalized knowledge, you become a well-rounded person. But it is the specialized knowledge that earns you your living. The question you should begin to ask yourself is, "What kind of knowledge do I possess, generalized knowledge or specialized knowledge?

It goes without saying that majority of Nigerian graduates, of whom I am one, have acquired nothing more than generalized knowledge. This is why the rate of unemployment is soaring higher with every passing year; and the labour market is getting more and more saturated with assortment of degrees, certificates and diplomas. But the earlier these well-meaning graduates dropped their load of certificates and begin to think of what specialized knowledge they can acquire in order to survive in this hostile society of ours, the better for them.

It is necessary to point out that the era of paper qualification is already on its way towards extinction. What we are approaching, or even in now, is the era of specialized knowledge; the era of personal skills; and the era of individual talents. In this 21st century, what matters most is not how many impressive certificates of generalized knowledge you are able to exhibit; rather, what is important is what you are able to do with the special knowledge that you have. In other words, your ability to survive now and in the very near future is dependent on your ability to acquire and organize a particular specialized knowledge for profitable use. Better still, your ability to identify your special skill(s) or your individual talent(s) and employ it (them) for profitable ventures will, no doubt, be the life saver in the emergent 21st century.

It is important that we conclude this chapter with an advice for he who has not lived up to the demands of wisdom. The advice is gleaned from the following words by Jonathan Swift: "The latter part of a wise man's life is taken up in curing the follies, prejudices, and false opinions he had contracted in the former." In other words, it is not too late for you to embrace wisdom. In fact, it is your ability to realize your follies and make a U-turn in midlife that makes you a wise person. And, as you begin to embrace wisdom, please start with your lips; for, "Every man shall kiss his lips that giveth a right answer. (Proverbs 24:26). Shalom!

11

The Purpose of Prosperity

Among spiritual leaders, inspirational writers and motivational speakers all over the world, it is common knowledge that when the purpose of a thing is not known, abuse becomes inevitable. Much as we emphasize the need for you to accumulate abundant financial wealth in this text, we must not fail to also ask you this very important question: What do you want to do with the money? Answering this question is compulsory, because it is devilish to have the desire to accumulate money just for the fun of it.

1 Timothy 6:10 says,

> For the love of money is the root of all evil: which while some coveted after, they have erred from the faith, and pierced themselves through with many sorrows.

Much of the atrocious evils committed by man on planet are traceable to man's insatiable and uncontrollable desire for money.

At the moment, the world is still bemoaning the scourge of the global economic melt-down or recession, global violence and wanton destruction of lives and properties that are ravaging the entire world. And the question that is on every lip is, "how do we get out of this mess?" But before we start talking about how to get out, I think it is necessary that we first address the question of how we got in. Just how did we get here? How did we get ourselves into this mess?

The Indian sage, Mahatma Ghandi, saw it coming when he ventured to voice out: *"There are seven (7) sins in the world: wealth without work; pleasure without conscience; knowledge without character; commerce without morality; science without humanity; worship without sacrifice; and politics without principle."* Obviously, a cursory look at the present human society is enough for one to see these seven societal ills starring back at us with all bestial glare. Everywhere in the human society, men are deviously all out to acquire wealth without work; they are running after pleasure with utmost recklessness; and people now go after knowledge without paying a modicum of attention to character. Go into the marketplace, and you will be shocked by how men listlessly sacrifice morality on the altar of commerce, as well as sell out humanity for a morsel of meal. Then, come to the religious circle and you will witness the most succinct epitome of worship without sacrifice – Men, these days, want to serve both God and mammon! We need not talk about the political scene; for, this is an arena for a free-for-all depravity. Yes, Ghandi saw it coming, and he made a rather faint and unheeded attempt to warn the world that was to come after him – our present world.

But Ghandi was not the only person who saw the handwriting on the wall. H.L. Menchen also saw what was soon to get the world into trouble, and he cried out: ***"It is not materialism that is the chief curse of the world, but idealism. Men get into trouble by taking their visions and hallucinations too seriously."*** It happened first around the eastern bloc, at the plain of Shinar, when men thought to build a city and a tower, whose top may reach unto heaven. It happened first when men conceived the idea and said, ***"Let us make us a name."*** It happened first at the time that God was made to come down from His heavenly throne to behold the site where men were labouring hard to maintain a global union that would ensure that they were not scattered abroad upon the face of the earth. Yes, it happened first when even the almighty God felt threatened by the fact: ***"the people is one, and they have all one language; and this they begin to do: and now nothing will be restrained from them, which they have imagined to do"*** (Genesis 11:1-9).

So, how did we get into this mess? Yes, we got into this global mess and menace because we started taking our visions and hallucinations too seriously. Of course, we have been bitten by the bug of materialism. But that is really not the biggest of human problems. The most deadly bug that is now sucking the lifeblood of humanity is that of idealism – the same problem that got the people of the Babel world into trouble with God. And who told you that the problem of the global economic recession that is currently plaguing the world is not a repeat of the Babel experience? Who told you that we are in this mess not because the world dreamt and has been labouring towards achieving political and economic union – what has been christened global security?

You are not duty bound to totally agree with me, as to the reason we are where we are now. But whether you agree with me or not, the fact remains that, for whatever reasons, we have landed ourselves in a mess that has graduated into a global menace, from which we must seek a way (or some ways) to get out.

There's More to Life than Having Everything

Surely, there's more to life than having everything. Right from the day of creation, the almighty God did not mean for man to have everything at the same time. Yes, God created all things in the world for the comfort of man. But He did not mean that man must lay hold on everything at any particular time. For any man to do this is to get choked out of existence. This is why God established boundaries and constraints for all of His creatures, including man.

Unfortunately, right from the days of Adam, man acquired the covetous nature that has given him the strong desire to have everything at the same time. This is responsible for the insatiable nature of man that has fired a quantum quantity of uncontrollable greed in him. And as it is today, man wants to grab and grab until there is nothing more to grab. And he does this with utmost disregard to the needs of his fellow man. Hence the average man in our present day society is very greedy and selfish. With this, it seems that the farther away we go from the Adamic age, ironically, the more depraved we grow; whereas, the reverse is supposed to be the case.

As we said in the first chapter of this text, the bug of materialism has bitten the men of this generation deeper than ever. And the effect is very conspicuous in the seven segments of Mahatma Gandhi's seven sins of the world.

But we must remind ourselves of the warning and teaching of our Lord and Saviour, Jesus Christ, "Take heed, and beware of coveteousness: for a man's life constisteth not in the abundance of things which he possesseth." (Luke 12:15). Really, it is not how much money or material things you accumulate that matters, but what you do with what you accumulate. If you gather and accumulate all the money in the world for yourself alone and you die today, the money will no longer be useful to you; it will go back into circulation in the world to be used by other people, with or without your consent. But by then you would have most probably lost your soul in hell. "For what is a man profited, if he shall gain the whole world, and lose his own soul or what shall a man give in exchange for his soul?" (Matthew 16:26). We must constantly remember that we brought nothing into this world, and it is certain that we shall take nothing out of it. Naked we came, and naked we shall return. (Job 1:21). Therefore we should learn and endeavor not to make mammon our god but to give money its proper perspective and to use our wealth to serve good purposes.

Some Good Uses of Money
1. Desire to do good and be a blessing – Money is a spiritual concept – it contains the power to do good, and to contribute to the development of the human society. Make a commitment to using your money to do good; to serve some worthy causes; to bless the less privileged members of the society; to serve or service the work of the kingdom of God; and to contribute to the development of your community, nation and the world at large.
2. Legacy for Beneficiaries – How would your children, grand children, great grand children, great great grand children – a century from now – benefit from your wise financial, spiritual and intellectual legacy? Proverbs 13:22 says, "A good man leaveth an inheritance to his children's children: and the wealth of the sinner is laid up for the just." This tells us that any man who lives his life selfishly without leaving anything behind for his children and children's children is a bad man. Therefore, you must think beyond yourself. If you won't save and accumulate wealth for yourself, at least do it for your beneficiaries. The single one naira (or dollar), money seed, that you sow today contains enormous power to bless you and countless future generations. So, start sowing your money seed now. Your future and the future of your children and children's children are counting on you. They are worth the sacrifice.

But this does not mean that we must steal and amass the wealth of the whole world for the purpose of leaving an inheritance for our children and children's children. There must be moderation in all things.

Let us consider, below, the example of some good Americans who amassed great wealth and are using their wealth to serve good and great purposes all over the world.

TOP TEN FOUNDATIONS IN THE U.S.
1. Bill & Melinda Gates Foundation $24, 082, 053, 000
2. Lilly Endowment Inc. $10, 054, 031, 550
3. The Ford Foundation (1936) $9, 300, 140, 000
4. J. Paul Getty Trust $8, 623, 795, 970
5. Robert Wood Johnson Foundation $8, 012, 367, 000
6. The David & Lucile Packard Foundation $6, 196, 520, 868
7. The William & Flora Hewlett Foundation $6, 080, 721, 309
8. W.K. Kellogg Foundation $5, 530, 494, 099
9. The Starr Foundation $4, 781, 056, 809
10. John D. & Catherine T. MacArthur F. $4, 215, 930, 831

The above figures represent the worth of the above foundations between 2001 and 2002, and they have been blessing hundreds of thousands of people (including you) each day over the years, and very many more people will continue to benefit from the legacy of these great money masters for generations to come, as they have continued to be channels of blessing to the whole world.

You can also go and do likewise, rather than live a selfish and self-centred life. Like these highly selfless money masters, you can establish a foundation through which other people can benefit from your wealth; you can give towards the building of the kingdom of God; you can give for the pursuit of a worthy cause; you can give to orphanages, old people's homes, refugee's centres, rehabilitation centres, etc. By doing so, you will establish a worthy legacy that will outlive you and continue to be a blessing to the world. This is the real purpose of prosperity.

12

It's A Covenant Walk

Prosperity, especially in the kingdom, is not so much a function of hard work, or of thrift, or of prudence, or of human wisdom, or of saving, or of prayer and fasting, or of faith. Engaging all of these factors is good; but if the right thing is not taken care of, all of these may end in futility and frustration. Prosperity is not so much about the efforts you make; rather, it is so much about the God that is at work in your life. Deuteronomy 8:18 says:

> But thou shalt remember the Lord thy God: for it is he that giveth thee power to get wealth, that he may establish his covenant which he sware unto thy fathers, as it is this day.

Prosperity is about the Lord your God who gives you the power to get wealth. You cannot get wealth until you are given the power to get it. So, if you like, work hard as you can; save as much as you can; pray and fast as much as you can; and even exercise as much faith as you can; if God has not given you the power to get wealth, you will never have it. Prosperity does not even come from abroad; it comes only from above; and it is God who gives the power to get it.

The reason why God gives His children the power to get wealth is because He desires to establish the covenant that He made with our fathers, Abraham, Isaac and Jacob.

> And when Abram was ninety years old and nine, the Lord appeared to Abram, and said unto him, I am the Almighty God; walk before me, and be thou perfect. And I will make my covenant between me and thee, and will multiply thee exceedingly.... As for me, behold, my covenant is with thee, and thou shalt be a father of many nations.... And I will make thee exceeding fruitful, and I will make nations out of thee, and kings shall come out of thee. And I will establish my covenant between me and thee and thy seed after thee in their generations for an everlasting covenant, to be a God unto thee and to thy seed after thee. And I will give unto thee, and to thy seed after thee, the land wherein thou art a stranger, all the land of Canaan, for an everlasting possessions; and I will be their God. And God said unto Abraham, Thou shalt keep my covenant therefore, thou, and thy seed after thee in their generations. (Genesis 17: 1-9).

After Abraham obeyed God by attempting to offer his only son, Isaac as sacrifice as God commanded him, God reinforced this covenant:

> And the angel of the Lord called unto Abraham out of heaven the second time, And said, By myself have I sworn, saith the Lord, for because thou hast done this thing, and hast not withheld thy son, thine only son: That in blessing I will thee, and in multiplying I will multiply thy seed as the stars of the heaven, and as the sand which is upon the sea shore; and thy seed shall possess the gate of his enemies; And in thy seed shall all the nations of the earth be blessed; because thou hast obeyed my voice. (Genesis 22:15-18).

As a result of this covenant, God greatly blessed Abraham in all things, and he became very rich in silver, gold, flocks and herds, camels and asses menservants and maidservants, wives, sons and daughters and with long life (Genesis 13 1-2; 24:1,35; 25:7-8).

After the death of Abraham, God reinforced his covenant with Isaac, his son:

> And the Lord appeared unto him, and said, Go not down into Egypt; dwell in the land which I shall tell thee of: Sojourn in this land, and I will be with thee, and I will bless thee; for unto thee, and unto thy seed, I will give all these countries, and I will perform the oath which I sware unto Abraham thy father: And I will make thy seed to multiply as the stars of heaven, and will give unto thy seed all these countries; and in thy seed shall

all the nations of the earth be blessed. Because that Abraham obeyed my voice, and kept my charge, my commandments, my statures, and my laws. (Genesis 26:2-5).

Thus, after the death of Abraham, this covenant found practical expression in the life of Isaac:

And it came to pass after the death of Abraham, that God blessed his son Isaac; and Isaac dwelt by the well of Lahairoi (Genesis 25:11).

Then Isaac sowed in that land, and received in the same year an hundredfold: and the Lord blessed him. And the man waxed great, and went forward, and grew until he became very great: For he had possession of flocks, and possessions of herds, and great store of servants: and the Philistines envied him. (Genesis 26:12-14).

This same covenant was reinforced by God and was practically expressed in the life of Jacob, the son of Isaac:

And, behold, the Lord stood above it, and said, I am the Lord God of Abraham thy father, and the God of Isaac: the land whereon thou liest, to thee will I give it, and to thy seed; And thy seed shall be as the dust of the earth, and thou shalt spread abroad to the west, and to the east, and to the north, and to the south: and in thee and in thy seed

> shall all the families of the earth be blessed. And, behold, I am with thee, and will keep thee in all places whither thou goest, and will bring thee again into this land; for I will not leave thee, until I have done that which I have spoken to thee of. (Genesis 28:13-15).

Consequently,

> ...the man increased exceedingly, and had much cattle, and maidservants, and menservants, and camels, and asses. (Genesis 30:43).

And of Esau and Jacob, Isaac's sons, it was said,

> Their riches were more than that they might dwell together; and the land wherein they were strangers could not bear them because of their cattle. (Genesis 36:7).

So, the covenant of prosperity that God made with Abraham has been speaking among the descendants of Abraham since the covenant was enacted in the Abrahamic age till date. And if you can recall very well, this covenant is an everlasting covenant that is meant to keep speaking among the seeds of Abraham from generation to generation forever.

> Now to Abraham and his seed were the promises made. He saith not, And to seeds, as of many; but as of one, and to thy seed, which is Christ. (Galatians 3:16)

What this simply means is that the promise which God made to Abraham when the covenant was enacted actually has its referent in Jesus Christ. In other words, Jesus Christ is the promised seed of Abraham that the covenant referred to, and not necessarily Isaac and other biological children of Abraham.

> And this I say, that the covenant, that was confirmed before of God in Christ, the law, which was four hundred and thirty years after, cannot disannul, that it should make the promise of none effect. For if the inheritance be of the law, it is no more of promise: but God gave it to Abraham by promise. (Galatians 3:17-18).

This means that what confirms the covenant is not the law but Jesus Christ, the promised seed of Abraham. The law was just a stop-gap measure that was meant to fill the void between when the promise was given to Abraham and when the promised seed, Jesus Christ, should come.

> Wherefore the law was our schoolmaster to bring us unto Christ, that we might be justified by faith. But after that faith is come, we are no longer under a schoolmaster. (Galatians 3:24-25).

Consequently, what gives potency to the covenant is not the law, but Jesus Christ. And the beneficiaries of the covenant are not exclusively the biological seeds of Abraham or citizens of the Jewish nation, but also all those who are connected to Abraham through faith in the promised seed, Jesus Christ.

> For ye are all the children of God by faith in Christ Jesus Christ. For as many of you as have been baptized into Christ have put on Christ. There is neither Jew nor Greek, there is neither bond nor free, there is neither male nor female: for ye are all one in Christ Jesus. And if ye be Christ's, then are ye Abraham's seed, and heirs according to the promise. (Galatians 3:26-29).

So what qualifies you, or any one for that matter, to enjoy the benefits of the promise of the covenant that God made with Abraham is faith in Christ Jesus. Until you have and exercise faith in Christ, and become born again, you are operating outside the covenant of blessings and prosperity that God enacted with Abraham. But the moment you become born again, your faith in Christ automatically connects you to the covenant, and it begins to speak or manifest in your life:

> Know ye therefore that they which are of faith, the same are the children of Abraham. And the scripture, foreseeing that God would justify the heathen through faith, preached before the gospel unto Abraham, saying, In thee shall all nations be blessed. So then they which be of faith are blessed with faithful Abraham. (Galatians 3:7-9).

The reason why the covenant of blessing and prosperity cannot speak in the life of a person who is not having faith in Christ Jesus, and who is not born, is due to the curse of the law that was placed on sin. Hence every sinner is operating under the law and under a curse:

> For as many as are of the works of the law are under the curse: for it is written, CURSED IS EVERY ONE THAT CONTINUETH NOT IN ALL THINGS WHICH ARE WRITTEN IN THE BOOK OF THE LAW TO DO THEM. And law is not of faith: but, THE MAN THAT DOETH THEM SHALL LIVE IN THEM. (Galatians 3:10- 12; Deuteronomy 27:26).

So, no matter the efforts that a person who is operating under the curse of the law and of sin, makes to break away from poverty and into prosperity, he cannot succeed in the true sense of it. His efforts can yield possible results only when the curse is broken from him. And the only condition for being free from the curse of the law and of sin is faith in Christ Jesus:

> Christ hath redeemed us from the curse of the law, being made a curse for us: for it is written, CURSED IS EVERY ONE THAT HANGETH ON A TREE: That the blessing of Abraham might come on the Gentiles through Jesus Christ; that we might receive the promise of the Spirit through faith. (Galatians 3:13-14).

Hence, becoming born again is not only for the purpose of seeing the kingdom of God, but also for the purpose of being free from the curse of sin, the curse of the law, and the curse of poverty; it is also for the purpose of enjoying the covenant of blessing and of prosperity. Until you exercise faith in Jesus Christ and become born again, Aluta Continua; your struggles with poverty, lack and want will continue.

Say with me, "God forbid!" and turn your life over to God, by confessing your sins to God and repenting of them, and professing faith in Christ Jesus. When you do this sincerely, you become born again, and you begin to swim in the ocean of blessings, prosperity and the abundant life.

There's Covenant Work to Do
But, hold it! Enjoying the provisions and benefits of the covenant, after you become born again, is not automatic. You still have a work to do.

> But thou shalt remember the Lord thy God: for it is he that giveth thee power to get wealth, that he may establish his covenant which he sware unto thy fathers, as it is this day.

You have the responsibility of remembering the Lord your God who gives you the power to get your wealth, while God has the responsibility of establishing the covenant of blessing that he swore to our covenant fathers. What this means is that, as God blesses and provides for us, we are expected to remember the Provider who gave us the power to get the wealth, and not consume everything on ourselves alone. Rather, we are expected to give a portion of what God has provided us for the advancement of His cause and kingdom on earth. Doing this would show that we recognize and appreciate the key role that God is playing in our prosperity.

Fortunately for us, God has not left us in the dark regarding the portion of our income that we are to give to Him for the advancement of His kingdom. This is why He instituted tithe as the just way through which all of His children that He blesses and provides for can acknowledge and show appreciation for God's role in their prosperity. Hence, tithing is a covenant obligation on everyone that is receiving blessings and provisions from God. Anyone, therefore, who is not paying tithe is simply saying that his blessings and provisions are not coming from God; or that he does not recognize God as the One that is blessing him and providing for him. In other words, the person is indirectly saying that he has a source of provision that is different from God; which is to say that the person is claiming to have another god who provides for him; in which case he is claiming to be an idolater. Another way of seeing or putting it is that the person is depending on his own power for his blessings and prosperity. And you and I know that nobody can help himself. If God does not help you, then you are completely helpless. Therefore to continue to receive the help of God, you must continue to acknowledge the help of God in your life by paying your tithe regularly. This is why the next section is devoted to the subject of faithfulness in tithe and offering.

Be Faithful in Tithing

Tithing is a practice that is ordained by God as a means of opening the windows of God's blessings for His children. In Malachi 3:10, God commands:

> Bring ye all the tithes into the storehouse, that there may be meat in mine house, and prove me now herewith, saith the Lord of hosts, if I will not open you the windows of heaven, and pour you a blessing, that there shall not be room enough to receive it.

To fail to pay your tithe is not only to rob God of His part in your income, but to also rob yourself of the blessings that come with the paying of tithe.

Every one of God's children is in partnership with God. The covenant relationship that God establishes with His people also implies a partnership relationship. And just as God works with His children in spiritual matters, so also He works with them in their material and financial undertakings. And it is through the institution of tithe that God condescends to identify with the material pursuits of His children. It is through the paying of tithe that a child of God also recognizes and identifies with his partnership relationship with the Almighty God. Therefore for him to refuse to pay tithe is to refute, reject and renounce this divine/human partnership, as well as to cause the mighty hands of God to be removed from his business and financial undertakings.

In various parts of the Bible, God has promised to bless the works of our hands. An instance is Deuteronomy 28:1-14. Verses 11 and 12 specifically say,

> And the LORD shall make thee plenteous in goods, in the fruit of thy body, and in the fruit of thy cattle, and in the fruit of thy ground, in the land which the LORD sware unto thy fathers to give thee. The Lord shall open unto thee his good treasure, the heaven to give the rain unto thy land in his season, and to bless all the work of thine hand: and thou shalt lend unto many nations, and thou shalt not borrow.

Another instance is Psalm 1:1-3:

> BLESSED IS the man that walketh not in the counsel of the ungodly, nor standeth in the way of sinners, not sitteth in the seat of the scornful. But his delight is in the law of the LORD; and in his law doth he meditate day and night. And he shall be like a tree planted by the rivers of water, that bringeth forth his fruit in his season; his leaf also shall not wither; and whatsoever he doeth shall prosper.

Ours is to work with our hands, and God's part is to bless the works of our hands. This is why we are told that except the Lord builds the house, they labour in vain that build it. Whatever we are doing for a living, if the Lord is not with us to bless it, we may just as well be labouring in vain; we may just be like Peter, toiling all night and yet catching nothing. For, it is only when the Lord comes into the scene and takes control of the situation that we can catch a multitude of blessings. And what brings the mighty hand and the presence of God into our businesses, more than anything else, is our faithfulness in paying our tithe. It is not that God is interested in our money, but He simply wants us to acknowledge His role in the success of our businesses, as well as recognize Him as a part-owner of our businesses. In the business world, every partner in business, however small his contributions, is legally entitled to some part of the profit made. And since God sees Himself as a partner and, in fact, the key-player in our businesses, He therefore, through the institution of tithe, lays a legal claim to a percentage (10%) of the profit or income of our businesses.

One thing every child of God should know is that there are two personalities that are clamouring to go into partnership with him: God on the one hand, and satan on the other hand. That is to say, it is either you allow God to work with you, or you give room to the devil to operate with you. When a Christian identifies with God through the paying of tithe, he gives God the full responsibility of not only blessing the work of his hands, but also of helping to keep 'deboli', the devourer and the destroyer, from operating in his territory. On the other hand, when a person refuses to pay his tithe, he does not only receive the curse of God for robbing Him, but he also opens the door very wide for the devourer to come into his territory to destroy the fruits of his ground, and his labour (Malachi 3:8-11). Every of God's children therefore has a choice to make; either to work with God, the Master-builder of our destiny, or to work with 'debolis', the devourer and destroyer of our God-given purpose. And it is the payment or non-payment of tithe that determines who he chooses.

Give Bountifully

Added to the issue of tithe is that of offering. Offering is what you give above the ten percent of your income. While the payment of tithe is compulsory, the giving of offering is not mandatory. Offering is what you give, as you will, in appreciation of the blessings of God upon your life. There is no stipulated amount or percentage of your income that you are to give as offering. You can decide not to give at all, and you can decide to give all that you have; you can decide to give little and you can decide to give much. The choice is yours.

But what we need to stress here is that the rate of your giving is directly proportional to the rate of your receiving. This is what we found in Luke 6:38,

> Give, and it shall be given unto you; good measure, pressed down, and shaken together, and running over, shall men give unto your bossom. For with the same measure that ye mete withal it shall be measured to you again.

Therefore any Christian who wants to receive abundance of God's blessings through men cannot but give, give and keep giving. This is the number one secret of prosperity. And this is also the number one power that breaks the yoke of poverty.

Proverbs 11:24 describes for us two men who are distinguished by the rate of their giving:

> There is that scattereth, and yet increaseth; and there is that withholdeth more than is meet, but it tendeth to poverty.

To the natural man, it is prudence to keep what one has for oneself; but the man who is spiritually enlightened, and who has a mature mind, knows that it is more blessed to give than to receive. He wiould not mind scattering all that he has among the less-privileged and the needy, as well as in the building of God's kingdom. But the end-result is that the person who keeps all that he has for himself will not have beyond that which he keeps; while the person who scatters all that he has around will be surprised to see the seeds he sowed germinate, grow and bear fruits; some thirty fold, some sixty and some a hundred fold. Poverty can never stand in the way of such a person who gives.

As you resolve to build an empire of wealth, the tendency is that you would want to become very thrifty, miserly and frugal. Yes, you would want to save virtually every Kobo that comes your way. But, much as we emphasize and encourage the practices of frugality, thrifty spending and systematic saving in order to succeed at building the coveted financial fortress, we, at the same time, discourage the habits of being miserly and stingy, as these will only place a limit on your chance of building an empire of wealth. You should therefore learn to give bountifully so that you can also reap bountifully. This is the essence of the covenant walk with God.

BOOKS BY THE SAME AUTHOR

Money Management/Wealth Building

- The Quickest and Smartest Way to Make Money
- Steps for Building an Empire of Wealth
- The One Dollar A Day Millionaire

Inspiration/Motivation

- A to Z of Success Secrets
- Why Angels Fly
- The Power to Turn Your Life Around
- Understanding the Seasons of Life
- Peak Performance: A Pocketbook for Academic Excellence
- How to Improve Your Self-Esteem and Communication Skills
- Pathway to Personal Progress

Academic

- English Language and Language Skills
- Language in Business Communication
- A Simple Approach to the Language of Literature
- Literature and Development: Perspectives from Stylistics

ABOUT THE BOOK

THE ONE DOLLAR A DAY MILLIONAIRE

Virtually everybody in the world wants to be a millionaire. But not everybody knows what it takes to be a millionaire.

The only way to become a millionaire is to get involved in playing the millionaire's game. It is the game of making money; it is the game of saving money; it is the game of investing money; it is the game of making your money and other people's money to work for you; and above all, it is the game of numbers, which showcases the miracle of compound interest.

The goal of this book is to give you some financial education and to get you to change your attitude towards money and how to save and invest it.

If I can get you to form the habit of saving and investing at least one dollar a day, I would have achieved my aim of writing this book, and I would be fulfilled as having impacted you and your future generations.

ABOUT THE AUTHOR

DR. LUCKY VINCENT is an academic and motivational writer, teacher, speaker, publisher and self-development expert who is charged with the task of helping to groom super successful people for the development of the human society in the 21st century and beyond.

The best graduating student of the Faculty of Arts and Social Sciences, Ambrose Alli University, Ekpoma (1995), Lucky Vincent (a.k.a. Vincent P.A. Obobolo) holds B.A. (Hons) English, M.A. English and PhD Linguistics (Stylistics). He is currently a lecturer in the Department of English Studies, University of Port Harcourt, Rivers State, Nigeria. With many academic and inspirational publications to his credit, and many more in the pipeline, Dr. Lucky Vincent is poised to storm the new millennium with a bang!

www.ingramcontent.com/pod-product-compliance
Lightning Source LLC
Chambersburg PA
CBHW020904180526
45163CB00007B/2621